# BURGER COOKERY

## by Pat Jester

# Contents

ANOTHER BEST-SELLING COOKERY VOLUME FROM H.P. BOOKS

Author: Pat Jester; Co-authors: Linda Welch, Joanne Johnson; Publisher: Helen Fisher; Editor: Carlene Tejada; Book Design: Don Burton; Book Assembly: Tom Jakeway; Typography: Connie Brown, Cindy Coatsworth; Food Stylists: Pat Jester, Linda Welch, Joanne Johnson; Photography: George deGennaro Studios—George deGennaro, David Wong, Dennis Skinner, Tom Miyasaki; Editor-in Chief: Carl Shipman.

**Published by H.P. Books, P.O. Box 5367, Tucson, AZ 85703 602/888-2150**

ISBN: Softcover, 0-89586-001-5; Hardcover, 0-89586-002-3
Library of Congress Catalog Card Number, 77-95176 © 1978 Fisher Publishing, Inc.
Printed in U.S.A.

## Pat Jester

Good food is what Pat Jester's life and work is all about. She is especially concerned with the quality of the food we eat and how to prepare and present it in the most appetizing ways.

Pat has been creating new recipes and improving old ones since her days at Iowa State University where she earned a degree in dietetics. From there Pat went on to dietary work in hospitals. She also did recipe development and food styling for the photography in various food and entertainment publications. The next phase of Pat's work was developing instruction books and sales literature for food appliances. This included extensive work with microwave ovens before her involvement with burger cookers. Pat writes a diet column for *Better Homes and Gardens,* and was formerly a food editor for that popular magazine.

At her own company, Creative Foods, Ltd., in Des Moines, Iowa, Pat develops and tests new recipes and does food styling for educational and advertising projects. Several well-known companies use Pat's expertise in their promotional booklets.

# How to Use Your Mini-Grill

Welcome to the world of convenience cookery! Your burger cooker is a versatile appliance. It's also called a *mini-grill* because it can cook just about anything in small amounts. Most of the recipes in this book will refer to your burger cooker as a *mini-grill* or a *grill*. If you're only interested in burgers, see pages 14 through 33. But if you want more taste adventures, try any of the more than 190 other ways to use your mini-grill. They will amaze you. This cookbook will help you enjoy good food, short cooking times and easy-to-follow recipes.

Whether you are a single person with a career, a busy working mother, a couple enjoying retirement, a student living away from home, or a homemaker with lots of people to cook for, you'll find uses for your handy mini-grill. Its small surface lends itself to easy cooking for the single person or the small family. Most large families eat in shifts—and you know how terrible cold, dried-out or burnt food tastes. With a mini-grill on your kitchen counter, you can get the food ready to cook ahead of time, then cook it whenever the dinner shift changes. Or you can let your family cook for themselves.

## Do's and Don'ts of Grilling

Plug electrical cord into grill before plugging into wall outlet.

Unplug cord and cool grill before cleaning.

Be careful removing hot grease or grease tray from grill.

Be careful removing or reversing the flip grids.

Clean the bottom tray of grill before storing.

Use utensils suitable for use on non-stick surfaces.

Keep grill well oiled to prevent food from sticking.

If food cooks too fast, unplug grill from wall outlet.

Use special cleaners designed for non-stick surfaces.

Don't clean grill while hot.

Don't use grill outdoors or on wet surfaces.

Don't operate grill with a damaged cord.

Don't immerse most grills in water for cleaning.

Don't let electrical cord hang over counter edge.

Don't leave grill plugged in when not in use.

Don't use grill on or near hot gas or electric burners.

Don't move grill when it contains hot oil or liquid.

Don't use grill for other than food preparation.

Don't place hot cover of grill on top of electrical cord.

Don't unplug electrical cord from grill before unplugging from wall.

The mini-grill is a great party tool, too. Here are 3 ways you can use it: You can prepare the snacks, appetizers, sandwiches, dinner or desserts on the mini-grill by yourself in the kitchen. Or you can prepare the food at the table in front of your guests. Or you can place the mini-grill with all the necessary ingredients right on the table and let your guests cook their own party dish.

You may find yourself owning this cookbook and not owning a mini-grill. Don't give the book away! These recipes can be used on any flat surface that will hold liquid and get hot enough to cook a steak. The skillet you use every day will do for most recipes.

There are burger cookers available which, because of their design, cannot be used as a mini-grill with the recipes in this book. Make sure the burger cooker you buy has a grill which will hold liquids. Many of the recipes in this book call for liquids, so this is an important feature.

## DOUBLE & SINGLE MINI-GRILLS

Basically there are 2 kinds of mini-grills: double grills and single grills. Double grills cook 2 hamburgers at once and usually hold about 2 cups of liquid. Single grills cook just 1 hamburger at a time and hold less liquid. The recipes in this cookbook were tested on a double grill. If you have a single grill, cut the recipes in half or cook in 2 batches.

## SERVING SIZES

Most of the recipes make 2 servings. If you want 4 servings with a 2 serving recipe, double the recipe and cook in 2 batches.

1/Open-Grill Cooking—This unit is prepared for open grilling. This particular unit stacks the lid with the heating element on top of the bottom grease tray, but this varies by manufacturer. Consult the use and care directions. Open grilling sometimes requires a heat-resistant surface.

2/Closed-Grill Cooking—Some units need to be placed on a heat-resistant surface because some mini-grills get hot enough to destroy fine finishes. If you have a choice of grid shapes, choose the one that best suits each recipe. Most grills have round grids to use for burgers and square grids for sandwiches. Others have lengthwise grids for hot dogs or large link sausage.

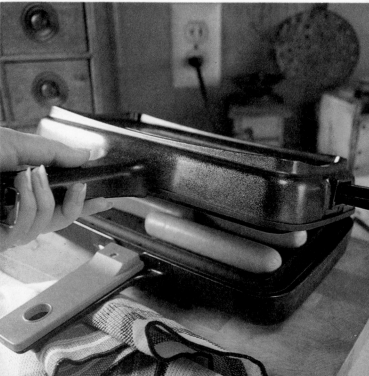

## PREHEATING TIME

When you use the mini-grill, allow for preheating time. Some of the grills warm up in 3 minutes or less while others need 10 minutes. Check the manufacturer's instructions or the Buyer's Guide in this book to find out what the preheating time is for your appliance. Take this into consideration before you begin a recipe.

## OPEN-GRILL COOKING

How you set up the unit for open grilling depends on which machine you own. *Consult the manufacturer's instructions before you start.* Because most grills have the heating element in the lid, this usually means cooking with the lid on a flat, dry, heat-resistant surface. Some units are stacked with the lid on top of the bottom for open grilling. When a recipe says "prepare unit for open grilling," follow your manufacturer's directions to the letter. Most grills require brushing with oil before cooking.

Be sure to plug the electrical cord into the grill first, then into the wall outlet.

**3/Seasoning the Grill—Most manufacturers recommend seasoning the grill with oil before using. You may need to add more oil during cooking to keep food from sticking. It is also helpful to brush the grill with oil after washing and drying so that it will be seasoned for the next use.**

**4/Cooking Speed—If a sauce is bubbling too vigorously or if spattering becomes excessive while frying foods, unplug the grill from the wall outlet. Let the grill cool a few minutes, then plug it back in. Because most grills do not have a temperature control, this is the only way to control the heat.**

## CLOSED-GRILL COOKING

For closed grilling, some units need to be on a flat, dry, heat-resistant surface. Follow the manufacturer's directions. Preheating times vary with different grills. Check the preheating time of your grill in the use and care directions. Some units require brushing with oil before cooking. You may have a choice of round or square grid shapes. Remember to plug the electrical cord into the grill first, then into the wall outlet.

## COOKING TECHNIQUES

Season the grill with oil according to the manufacturer's instructions. If necessary, add more oil during cooking to prevent food from sticking.

If foods are cooking too fast or a sauce is boiling too hard, unplug the grill by removing the electrical cord from the wall outlet for a few minutes. When cooking has slowed sufficiently, plug the grill back in and continue cooking.

Stir foods from the outside edges toward the center because the food along the edges is usually nearer the heating element and cooks much faster.

You don't have to clean the grill between cooking meats or vegetables and making gravy or a sauce to go with them. The bits of food and drippings left on the grill add flavor to the sauce. The recipes in

5/Stirring Foods—For more even cooking, stir food from the outside edges toward the center. This is especially important when you are thickening sauces. The heating element is usually located near the edges so food near the edge cooks much faster.

6/Cleaning the Grill—Use soapy water and a sponge or scrubber for non-stick surfaces. Most grills should not be immersed in water. Unplug the electrical cord from the wall outlet and then from the grill before washing. Special commercial cleaners are available for stubborn stains.

this book will tell you when it's necessary to clean the mini-grill if more than 1 item is to be made.

The timings in these recipes are estimates meant to serve as a guideline. These timings will vary slightly with different grills. Cooking times may also be affected by voltage differences at times of peak power demands.

*Never leave your mini-grill plugged in when you have finished cooking.*

## LIQUID CAPACITY

The double grills used for testing recipes in this book held about 2 cups of liquid. But grill capacities vary. Use your judgment when pouring liquid onto the grill. It's a good idea to test the liquid capacity of your grill by pouring a measured amount of water onto the grill. Then you can make any needed adjustments in the recipes.

## WASHING THE GRILL

When you are through cooking, unplug the electrical cord from the wall outlet and then from the grill. Let the grill cool before washing.

Most grills are not immersible, so do not plunge yours into a sink filled with water. To clean the cooking surface, use soapy water and a sponge or scrubber especially designed to clean non-stick surfaces. To remove stubborn foods, place 1/2 cup cold water on the cold grill, plug in the grill and bring the water to a boil. Let the water cool, empty the grill and wipe off the loosened food particles. To prevent foods from sticking, oil the grill between uses.

After long continued use of your mini-grill, you may need to use a commercial cleaner developed especially for use on non-stick surfaces. These are usually available at your supermarket or department store.

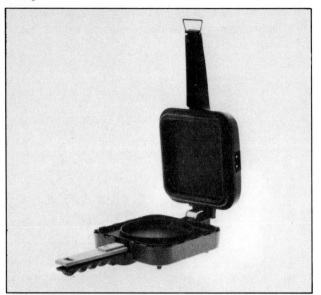

**Great American Burger Machine**
American Electric, Culver City, CA 90230
**Preheating Time:** 5 minutes     **Grill Size:** 4-1/2'' x 4-1/2'' x 1/2''
**Grill Capacity:** 1 cup     **Wattage:** 350 watts
The Great American Burger Machine is a single grill with a reversible, non-stick cooking grid. The top cover fits into bottom tray for open grilling. The grease tray and reversible grid are both immersible, but grill is not immersible.

**Great American Grilling Machine**
American Electric, Culver City, CA 90230
**Preheating Time:** 10 minutes     **Grill Size:** 9-1/2'' 7'' x 3/4''
**Grill Capacity:** 3 cups     **Wattage:** 700 watts
The Great American Grilling Machine is a double grill with a non-stick cooking surface. The reversible non-stick grid can be placed on top of the foods being cooked. It has a heat control with 4 settings. The grill does not have drain holes. The grid is immersible, but grill is not immersible.

**Lil Grill**
Farberware® Bronx, New York 10461
**Preheating Time:** 4 minutes     **Grill Size:** 4-1/2'' x 4-1/2'' x 1/2''
**Grill Capacity:** 1 cup     **Wattage:** 400 watts
Lil Grill is a single grill with a reversible non-stick cooking grid. The grill fits into bottom grease tray for open grilling; heat-resistant surface not required. Reversible grid and grease tray are immersible, but grill is not immersible.

**Lil Grill 2**
Farberware® Bronx, New York 10461
**Preheating Time:**                    Grill Size: 9-1/2'' x 4-3/4'' x 1/2''
   3 minutes—open grilling
   6 minutes—closed grilling
**Grill Capacity:** 2 cups          **Wattage:** 750 watts
Lil Grill 2 is a double grill with reversible, non-stick cooking surface. The non-stick grill fits into bottom grease tray for open grilling; heat-resistant surface not required. Reversible grid and grease tray are immersible, but grill is not.

**Frank-N-Burger<sup>T</sup> grill**
General Electric, Bridgeport, CT 06602
**Preheating Time:** 4 to 5 minutes   **Grill Size:** 5-1/4'' x 4-1/2'' x 1/2''
**Grill Capacity:** 1 cup          **Wattage:** 510 watts
The Frank-N-Burger$^T$ grill is a single grill with a reversible, non-stick cooking grid. The non-stick grill fits on bottom grease tray for open grilling; heat-resistant surface is not required. The bottom grease tray and grid are both immersible, but grill is not immersible. Hole in handle facilitates hanging storage.

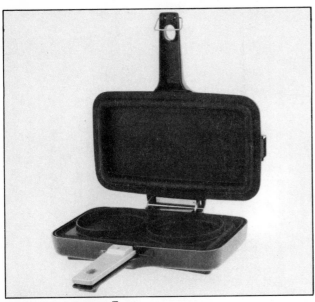

**SUPER Frank-N-Burger$^T$ grill**
General Electric, Bridgeport, CT 06602
**Preheating Time:** 5 minutes      **Grill Size:** 9'' x 4-1/4'' x 1/2''
**Grill Capacity:** 2 cups          **Wattage:** 750 watts
The Frank-N-Burger$^T$ grill is a double grill with a reversible, non-stick cooking grid. The non-stick grill fits on bottom grease tray for open grilling; heat resistant surface is not required. The bottom grease tray and grid are both immersible, but grill is not immersible. Hole in handle facilitates hanging storage.

**Double MAC**
Hamilton Beach, Div. of Scovill, Waterbury, CT 06720
**Preheating Time:** 5 to 6 minutes **Grill Size:** 9" x 4-1/2" x 5/8"
**Grill Capacity:** 2 cups **Wattage:** 700 watts
The Double MAC is a double grill with a reversible, non-stick cooking grid. "Legs" on cover eliminate the need for heat-resistant surface when open grilling. Grill has a non-stick finish. The bottom grease tray and grid are both immersible, but grill is not immersible.

**Little MAC**
Hamilton Beach, Div. of Scovill, Waterbury, CT 06720
**Preheating Time:** **Grill Size:** 4-1/2" x 4-1/2" x 1/2"
 3 to 5 minutes—open grilling
 5 minutes—closed grilling
**Grill Capacity:** 7/8 cup **Wattage:** 400 watts
The Little MAC is a single grill with a reversible, non-stick cooking grid. The non-stick grill fits into bottom grease tray for open grilling; heat-resistant surface is not required. The bottom grease tray and grid are both immersible, but grill is not immersible.

**Mighty Mac™**
MacDonald's Home Products, Sparta, MI 49345
**Preheating Time:** 3 minutes **Grill Size:** 9-1/4" x 4-1/2" x 3/4"
**Grill Capacity:** 2-1/4 cups **Wattage:** 800 watts
The Mighty Mac™ is a double grill with a reversible, "natural as-cast aluminum" cooking grid and grill. Grill can be placed directly on counter top for open grilling. Bottom grease tray and grid are both immersible, but grill is not immersible.

**Mighty Mac II**
MacDonald's Home Products, Sparta, MI 49345
**Preheating Time:** 3 minutes **Grill Size:** 9-1/4" x 4-1/2" x 3/4"
**Grill Capacity:** 2-1/4 cups **Wattage:** 800 watts
The Mighty Mac II is a double grill with a reversible, "natural as-cast aluminum" cooking grid. The grill is coated with a DuPont Silver Stone® non-stick finish and can be placed directly on counter top for open grilling. The bottom grease tray and grid are both immersible, but grill is not immersible.

**Burger Cooker™**
Norelco, North American Phillips, New York, NY 10017
**Preheating Time:** 5 minutes     **Grill Size:** 9″ x 4-1/2″ x 3/4″
**Grill Capacity:** 2 cups     **Wattage:** 800 watts
The Burger Cooker™ is a double grill with a reversible, non-stick cooking grid. One side of grid is slotted, which is useful for cooking hot dogs. The non-stick grill fits into bottom grease tray for open grilling; heat resistant surface is not required. The bottom grease tray and grid are both immersible, but grill is not immersible.

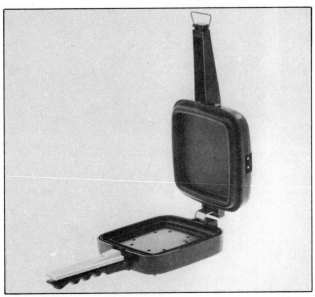

**Master Chef**
Northern Electric, Chicago, IL 60625
**Preheating Time:**     **Grill Size:** 4-1/2″ x 4-1/2″ x 1/2″
    1 to 2 minutes—open grilling
    5 minutes—closed grilling
**Grill Capacity:** 1 cup     **Wattage:** 400 watts
The Master Chef is a single grill with a reversible, non-stick cooking grid. "Legs" on non-stick grill eliminate the need for a heat resistant surface. Cooking grid and grease tray are both immersible, but grill is not immersible.

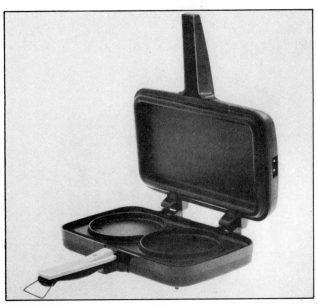

**Master Chef**
Northern Electric, Chicago, IL 60625
**Preheating Time:** 2 to 3 minutes     **Grill Size:** 9″ x 4-1/2″ x 3/4″
**Grill Capacity:** 2 cups     **Wattage:** 700 watts
The Master Chef is a double grill with a reversible, non-stick cooking grid. "Legs" on non-stick grill eliminate the need for a heat-resistant surface. Cooking grid and grease tray are both immersible, but grill is not immersible.

**SIZZ'L gril™**
Oster Corporation, Milwaukee, WI 53217
**Preheating Time:** 5 minutes     **Grill Size:** 5-3/4″ x 4-1/2″ x 7/8″
**Grill Capacity:** 1-1/2 cups     **Wattage:** 400 watts
The SIZZ'L gril™ is a large single grill with a reversible, non-stick cooking grid. Heat-resistant surface is required for open grilling on non-stick grill. Cover design allows holding it in an upright position when opened. The bottom grease tray base and cooking plate are both immersible, but grill is not immersible.

**SIZZ'L gril 2**
Oster Corporation, Milwaukee, WI 53217
**Preheating Time:** 8 minutes     **Grill Size:** 9-1/4'' x 4-3/4'' x 1/2''
**Grill Capacity:** 2 cups     **Wattage:** 725 watts
The SIZZ'L gril II is a double grill with a reversible, non-stick cooking plate. Heat-resistant surface is required for open grilling on non-stick grill. Cover design allows holding it in an upright position when opened. Red "Ready Dot" turns black when unit has preheated. The bottom grease tray base and cooking plate are both immersible, but grill is not immersible.

**Presto Burger™**
National Presto Industries, Eau Claire, WI 54701
**Preheating Time:** 4 to 5 minutes   **Grill Size:** 4 inches, round
**Grill Capacity:** 7/8 cup     **Wattage:** 400 watts
The Presto Burger™ is a single grill with a non-stick cooking tray. The non-stick grill must be placed on a heat-resistant surface for open grilling. The bottom drip pan and cooking tray are both immersible, but grill is not immersible.

**Presto Burger/1™ Liddle Griddle™**
National Presto Industries, Eau Claire, WI 54701
**Preheating Time:** 5 minutes     **Grill Size:** 4-1/4'' x 4-1/4'' x 5/8''
**Grill Capacity:** 1 cup     **Wattage:** 400 watts
The Presto Burger/1™ is a single grill with a reversible, non-stick, THICKnTHIN™ cooking tray. The non-stick Liddle Griddle™ grill must be placed on a heat-resistant surface for open grilling. The bottom drip pan and cooking tray are both immersible, but grill is not immersible.

**Presto Burger/2™ Liddle Griddle™**
National Presto Industries, Eau Claire, WI 54701
**Preheating Time:** 5 minutes     **Grill Size:** 8-3/4'' x 4-1/4'' x 5/8''
**Grill Capacity:** 1-3/4 cups     **Wattage:** 650 watts
The Presto Burger/2™ is a double grill with a reversible, non-stick, THICKnTHIN™ cooking tray. The non-stick Liddle Griddle™ grill must be placed on a heat-resistant surface for open grilling. The bottom drip pan and cooking tray are both immersible, but grill is not immersible.

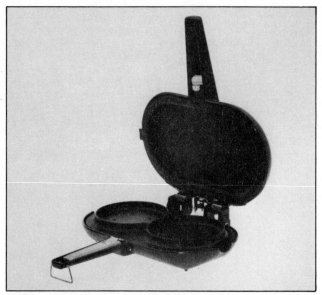

**Sizzler**
Toastmaster, McGraw-Edison, Columbia, MO 65201
**Preheating Time:**      **Grill Size:** 8-3/4'' x 4-1/4'' x 1/2''
    2 minutes—open grilling
    4 minutes—closed grilling
**Grill Capacity:** 1-3/4 cups    **Wattage:** 800 watts
The sizzler is a double grill with a reversible, non-stick cooking grid. The non-stick grill fits into bottom grease tray for open grilling; heat-resistant surface is not required. For closed grilling, cover can be locked in an upright position when opened. Except for the control probe, the unit is completely immersible.

**Mr. Burger 1, Catalog No. 34K6533**
Sears, Chicago, IL 60684
**Preheating Time:** 3 to 5 minutes  **Grill Size:** 4-1/2'' x 4-1/2'' x 1/2''
**Grill Capacity:** 7/8 cup    **Wattage:** 400 watts
The Mr. Burger 1 is a single grill with a reversible non-stick cooking grid. The non-stick grill fits into bottom grease tray. For open grilling, heat-resistant surface is not required. The bottom grease tray and grid are both immersible, but grill is not immersible. Appears to be similar to Hamilton Beach Little Mac.

**Mr. Burger 2, Catalog No. 34K6534**
Sears, Chicago, IL 60684
**Preheating Time:** 5 to 6 minutes  **Grill Size:** 9'' x 4-1/2'' x 5/8''
**Grill Capacity:** 2 cups    **Wattage:** 700 watts
The Mr. Burger 2 is a double grill with a reversible, non-stick cooking grid. "Legs" on cover eliminate the need for heat-resistant surface for open grilling. Grill has a non-stick finish. The bottom grease tray and grid are both immersible, but grill is not immersible. Appears to be similar to Hamilton Beach Double Mac.

**Wards Burger Cooker, Catalog No. 86A46014**
Montgomery Ward, Chicago, Il 60671
**Preheating Time:** 5 minutes    **Grill Size:** 4-1/4'' x 4-1/4'' x 5/8''
**Grill Capacity:** 1 cup    **Wattage:** 400 watts
The square Wards Cooker is a single grill with a reversible, non-stick cooking tray. The grill must be placed on a heat-resistant surface for open grilling. The bottom drip pan and cooking tray are both immersible, but grill is not immersible. Appears to be similar to Presto Burger 1 ™.

**Wards Burger Cooker, Catalog No. 86A46016**
Montgomery Ward, Chicago, IL 60671
**Preheating Time:** 5 minutes    **Grill Size:** 8-3/4'' x 4-1/4'' x 5/8''
**Grill Capacity:** 1-3/4 cups    **Wattage:** 650 watts
The Wards Double grill has a non-stick, reversible cooking tray. The non-stick grill must be placed on a heat-resistant surface for open grilling. The bottom drip pan and cooking tray are both immersible, but grill is not immersible. Appears to be similar to Presto Burger 2™.

**Wards Burger Cooker, Catalog No. 86A46009**
Montgomery Ward, Chicago, IL 60671
**Preheating Time:** 4 to 5 minutes  **Grill Size:** 4 inches, round
**Grill Capacity:** 7/8 cup    **Wattage:** 400 watts
The round Wards Cooker is a single grill with a non-stick cooking tray. The non-stick grill must be placed on a heat-resistant surface for open grilling. The bottom drip pan and cooking tray are both immersible, but grill is not immersible. Appears to be similar to round Presto Burger™.

**Automatic Twin Burger**
Black Angus
Winsted, CT 06098

The Automatic Twin Burger has 2 removable non-stick grids. This unit is designed to cook hamburgers, sandwiches and waffles. It can be used for some open grilling. Do not use recipes that require liquids to be poured into the grill.

**Double Burger/Plus**
Rival®
Kansas City, MO 64129

The Double Burger/Plus has 3 non-stick removable grids. This unit is designed to cook hamburgers, sandwiches and waffles. It can be used for some open grilling. Do not use recipes that require liquids to be poured into the grill.

**Superlectric Twin Burger**
Superior Electric Products
Cape Girardeau, MO 63701

The Superlectric Twin Burger has 3 non-stick removable grids. This unit is designed to cook hamburgers, sandwiches and waffles. It can be used for some open grilling. Do not use recipes that require liquids to be poured into the grill.

**Sunbeam 1 or 2**
Sunbeam, Oakbrook, IL 60521

Sunbeam 1 or 2 burger maker is designed to stack 1 or 2 hamburgers or sandwiches for closed grilling. It has 3 non-stick grids. The center grid contains the heating unit and is not immersible. The top and bottom grids and the drip tray are immersible. Do not use recipes that require liquid to be poured into the grill.

**Wiz Grid**
Mirro Matic, Mirro Aluminum, Manitowac, WI 54220

Mirro Matic Whiz Grid is designed for closed grilling. The non-stick grill is for hamburgers, sandwiches, steak, bacon or frankfurters. Do not use recipes that require liquid to be poured into the grill.

# *Burgers*

Versatile hamburger is even more versatile with a mini-grill. You can make it any way you want. Let your imagination soar. To make an instant burger, place 4 ounces of meat on the round grid side of the grill, close lid, *latch handle* and cook for 3 to 4 minutes. For more even browning you can turn the patty over halfway through the cooking time. If you don't care if the bottom side is less brown, don't bother to turn it.

To make thicker burgers or stuffed burgers, shape them and cook on the open grill or use the rectangular side of the grid in the closed grill. This keeps the filling from squishing out and promotes even cooking. Keep in mind that stuffed burgers, such as Green Goddess Burgers, take longer to cook than unstuffed ones.

The possibilities for jazzing up a plain burger are endless. First of all think of the choice of rolls and breads you have. Then consider all the vegetables, like lettuce, tomato, cucumber, bean sprouts, onion and mushrooms, that can enhance the burger's beefy flavor. You can add a slice or a sprinkle of your favorite cheese. And all those toppings! Chip dip, relish, pickles, mustard, horseradish and steak sauce are only a few. Buy something already prepared or make your own. Herb-Butter Toppings can make a plain hamburger into a gourmet delight.

When company comes, show off with Tostada Burgers with all the south-of-the-border trimmings, or turn ordinary hamburger into unforgettable Easy Beef Wellington.

Hamburger never had it so good. And neither have you!

# Filled Hamburgers

*Cheese-filled burgers will become a tradition at your house.*

8 oz. ground beef
1 egg, slightly beaten
1 tablespoon fine dry breadcrumbs
2 teaspoons dehydrated minced onion flakes
1/4 teaspoon salt

1/4 teaspoon Worcestershire sauce
Dash pepper
1/4 (3-oz.) pkg. cream cheese, softened
2 teaspoons crumbled blue cheese

Prepare unit for open grilling. In a medium bowl, mix beef, egg, breadcrumbs, onion flakes, salt, Worcestershire sauce and pepper. Shape into 4 thin patties. In a small bowl, combine cream cheese and blue cheese. Spoon cheese mixture onto 2 patties, spreading to within 1/2 inch of edges. Top with remaining patties; seal edges with fingertips. Cook patties on preheated grill until brown, about 3 to 4 minutes on each side. Makes 2 patties.

# Rarebit Burgers

*A triple treat: great for lunch, dinner or a snack.*

8 oz. ground beef
Salt and pepper to taste

1 English muffin, split
Savory Sauce, see below

*Savory Sauce:*
1/2 cup milk
1 tablespoon all-purpose flour
1 cup shredded sharp process cheese (4 oz.)
1/2 teaspoon dry mustard

1/2 teaspoon Worcestershire sauce
Dash bottled hot pepper sauce
1 egg yolk, beaten

Prepare unit for closed grilling. Shape beef into 2 patties. Sprinkle with salt and pepper. Place on preheated grill. Close lid; latch handle. Cook until brown, about 2 minutes on each side. Place cooked patties on muffin halves and keep warm. Clean grill. Prepare Savory Sauce. Spoon sauce over patties. Makes 2 open-face burgers.

Savory Sauce:
Prepare unit for open grilling. In a small bowl, mix milk and flour to make a paste. Pour onto cold grill; add cheese. Plug in grill. Cook and stir until cheese melts, about 1-1/2 minutes. Unplug grill; stir in mustard, Worcestershire sauce and hot pepper sauce. Stir a small amount of hot sauce into egg. Stir egg mixture back into mixture on grill. Plug in grill. Cook and stir until mixture thickens, about 1 minute. Makes about 1 cup sauce.

# Italian Hamburgers on Spaghetti

*Twirl this around your fork and enjoy the spicy flavor.*

8 oz. ground beef
2 oz. mild Italian sausage
1/2 cup soft breadcrumbs (1-1/2 slices bread)
1 egg, slightly beaten
2 tablespoons finely chopped onion
2 tablespoons tomato juice

1/2 teaspoon salt
1/8 teaspoon Italian seasoning
1/2 (15-oz.) jar spaghetti sauce
4 oz. spaghetti, cooked
Grated Parmesan cheese

Prepare unit for open grilling. In a medium bowl, mix beef, sausage, breadcrumbs, egg, onion, tomato juice, salt and Italian seasoning. Shape into 2 patties. Cook on preheated grill until brown, 3 to 4 minutes on each side. Remove and keep warm. Heat spaghetti sauce on grill 1 to 2 minutes. On a large plate, toss sauce with cooked spaghetti. Place patties on top of spaghetti; sprinkle with Parmesan cheese. Makes 2 servings.

# Pizza Burgers

*Quick and easy main dish with an immense fan club.*

8 oz. ground beef
1/8 teaspoon garlic salt
Dash pepper

2 slices cheese
2 large French rolls, halved lengthwise
Pizza Sauce, see below

*Pizza Sauce:*
1 (8-oz.) can tomato sauce
1/2 small onion, thinly sliced and separated
  into rings

2 tablespoons mushroom slices
1/4 teaspoon ground oregano

Prepare unit for closed grilling. In a medium bowl, mix beef, garlic salt and pepper. Shape into 2 patties. Place on preheated grill. Close lid; latch handle. Cook until brown, about 2 minutes on each side. Top each patty with a slice of cheese. Cut each patty in half and place 2 halves on each roll. Keep warm while making Pizza Sauce. Spoon sauce over patties. Makes 2 servings.

Pizza Sauce:
Prepare unit for open grilling. Place tomato sauce, onion, mushrooms and oregano on preheated grill. Cook and stir until boiling, about 1-1/2 minutes. Continue to cook and stir until onion is crisp-tender, about 2-1/2 minutes. Makes about 1-1/2 cups sauce.

# Cheese & Chili-Stuffed Burgers

*Double burgers with a surprise filling!*

8 oz. ground beef
1 tablespoon finely chopped onion
1/4 teaspoon salt
1/8 teaspoon chili powder

Dash pepper
1/2 cup shredded Cheddar cheese (2 oz.)
1 tablespoon canned chopped green chilies
2 hamburger rolls

Prepare unit for open grilling. In a medium bowl, mix beef, onion, salt, chili powder and pepper. Shape into 4 thin patties. Top 2 of the patties with cheese and chilies. Cover with remaining patties; seal edges with fingertips. Cook on preheated grill until brown, 3 to 4 minutes on each side. Serve on hamburger rolls. Makes 2 burgers.

# Taco Burgers

*Just a little Mexican spice.*

8 oz. ground beef
1 tablespoon chopped onion
1 tablespoon taco seasoning mix
1/4 teaspoon salt
1/4 teaspoon Worcestershire sauce

Dash pepper
1/2 cup shredded Cheddar cheese (2 oz.)
1/2 cup shredded lettuce
1/2 tomato, chopped
2 hamburger rolls

Prepare unit for closed grilling. In a medium bowl, mix beef, onion, seasoning mix, salt, Worcestershire sauce and pepper. Shape into 2 patties. Place on preheated grill. Close lid; latch handle. Cook until browned, about 2 minutes on each side. Top with cheese, lettuce and tomato. Serve on hamburger rolls. Makes 2 burgers.

# Tostada Burgers

*Keep the kids home for dinner with this tempting burger!*

1/2 cup refried beans
1 tablespoon taco seasoning mix
2 tostada shells
1 (8-oz.) can mixed vegetables, drained
2 tablespoons red wine salad dressing
1/2 teaspoon chili powder

8 oz. ground beef
Crisp lettuce leaves
2 slices tomato
Shredded process American cheese
Taco sauce
Pickled chili peppers

Prepare unit for closed grilling. In a small bowl, mix beans and seasoning mix; spread on tostada shells. In another small bowl, mix vegetables, salad dressing and chili powder; spoon over beans on shells. Shape beef into 2 patties. Place on preheated grill. Close lid; latch handle. Cook until brown, about 2 minutes on each side. Place patties on top of vegetables. Top with lettuce, tomato and cheese. Serve with taco sauce and chili peppers. Makes 2 open-face burgers.

# Sesame Burgers

*Sesame seed gives unusual flavor and crunchy texture.*

8 oz. ground beef
2 tablespoons toasted sesame seed
1-1/2 teaspoons soy sauce
1/4 teaspoon salt

Dash pepper
2 slices pineapple
2 hamburger rolls

Prepare unit for closed grilling. In a medium bowl, mix beef, sesame seed, soy sauce, salt and pepper. Shape into 2 patties. Place on preheated grill. Close lid; latch handle. Cook until brown, about 2 minutes on each side. Top with pineapple slices. Serve on hamburger rolls. Makes 2 burgers.

**Tostada Burger**

# Blue Cheese Burgers

*Bacon, blue cheese and sour cream add elegance to a quick burger.*

8 oz. ground beef
1-1/2 teaspoons bacon bits
1/4 teaspoon salt
Dash pepper

1/4 cup dairy sour cream
1 tablespoon crumbled blue cheese
1-1/2 teaspoons finely chopped green onion
2 hamburger rolls

Prepare unit for closed grilling. In a medium bowl, mix beef, bacon bits, salt and pepper. Shape into 2 patties. Place on preheated grill. Close lid; latch handle. Cook until brown, about 2 minutes on each side. In a small bowl, mix sour cream, blue cheese and green onion. Spoon on cooked patties. Serve on hamburger rolls. Makes 2 burgers.

# Spud Burgers

*Take meat and potatoes out of the pot, give them a new shape and serve in a bun.*

8 oz. ground beef
1 small potato, peeled and finely grated
2 tablespoons finely chopped onion

1/2 teaspoon salt
2 slices American cheese
2 hamburger rolls

Prepare unit for closed grilling. In a medium bowl, mix beef, potato, onion and salt. Shape into 2 patties. Place on preheated grill. Close lid, but do not latch handle. Cook until brown, 2 to 3 minutes on each side. Top with cheese slices. Serve on hamburger rolls. Makes 2 burgers.

# Slaw Burgers

*Creamy cole slaw dresses these nippy burgers on rye toast.*

1/4 cup shredded cabbage
1 tablespoon shredded carrot
1 tablespoon chopped radish
1/4 teaspoon celery seed

1/2 cup Neufchatel dip with horseradish and
  bacon
8 oz. ground beef
2 slices rye toast

Prepare unit for closed grilling. In a small bowl, mix cabbage, carrot, radish and celery seed. Toss with 1/4 cup of the dip; chill. In a medium bowl, combine remaining dip and beef; mix well. Shape into 2 patties. Place on preheated grill. Close lid; latch handle. Cook until brown, about 2 minutes on each side. Serve open-face on rye toast. Top with chilled cole slaw. Makes 2 open-face burgers.

# Easy Beef Wellington

*No one said it would be easy—until now!*

8 oz. ground beef
Garlic salt
1 tablespoon butter or margarine
1 (4-oz.) tube refrigerated crescent rolls

1 (3-oz.) can mushroom slices, drained
Garlic salt
1 tablespoon vegetable oil

Prepare unit for open grilling. Shape beef into 2 patties. Sprinkle with garlic salt. Melt butter or margarine on preheated grill. Add patties and cook until light brown and still rare, about 2 minutes on each side. On a generously floured surface, roll out 2 crescent rolls to form one 7-inch square. Repeat with remaining 2 crescent rolls. Spoon mushrooms onto center of each square; sprinkle wtih garlic salt. Place patties on top of mushrooms. Fold dough over patties and seal with fingertips. Add oil to grill. Place burger bundles on grill and cook until golden brown on all sides, about 1 minute on each side. Turn on edge to cook evenly around the edges. Makes 2 servings.

## How to Make Easy Beef Wellington

**1/**Roll 2 refrigerated crescent rolls on a floured surface to a 7-inch square. Spoon mushrooms onto center of dough and sprinkle with garlic salt.

**2/**Place precooked burger on top of mushrooms. Fold corners of dough over burger and seal. Cook in hot oil on grill, turning for even cooking, until golden brown.

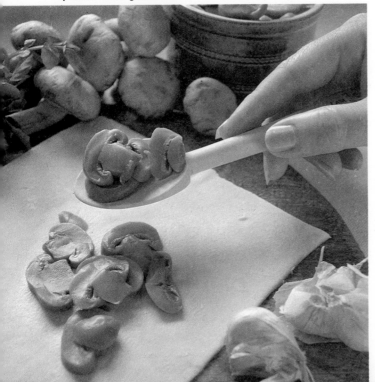

# Bacon Burgers

*A bacon design provides an elegant touch.*

4 slices bacon
8 oz. ground beef
1/3 cup shredded Cheddar cheese (1-1/3 oz.)
1 egg, slightly beaten
2 tablespoons water

1 tablespoon fine dry breadcrumbs
1/2 teaspoon dehydrated minced onion flakes
1/4 teaspoon salt
1/8 teaspoon instant beef bouillon granules
2 hamburger rolls

Prepare unit for open grilling. On preheated grill, partially cook bacon, being careful to keep it limp and not crisp, 2-1/2 to 3-1/2 minutes. Set bacon aside and drain grill. In a medium bowl, mix beef, cheese, egg, water, breadcrumbs, onion flakes, salt and bouillon granules. Shape into 2 patties. Wrap 2 bacon slices around each patty, making an X. Cook patties on grill until brown, about 3 minutes on each side. Serve on hamburger rolls. Makes 2 burgers.

# Dilly Zucchini Burgers

*Make tasty relish from your bumper zucchini crop.*

3 tablespoons cider vinegar
1 tablespoon sugar
1 tablespoon water
1/4 teaspoon celery salt
1/4 cup thin zucchini slices
1 tablespoon chopped green onion

1 tablespoon parsley flakes
1/2 teaspoon dried dillweed
8 oz. ground beef
2 tablespoons chopped dill pickle
2 whole-wheat hamburger rolls

In a small bowl, combine vinegar, sugar, water and celery salt. Mix well. Add zucchini, onion, parsley and dillweed; toss to coat. Refrigerate for 2 hours. Prepare unit for closed grilling. Shape ground beef into 2 patties. Place on grill. Close lid; latch handle. Cook until brown, about 2 minutes on each side. Drain zucchini relish. Stir in chopped dill pickle. Serve burgers on rolls and top with relish. Makes 2 servings.

---

*Grills may lose some of their non-stick finish after they become well-used. Try spraying with a non-stick spray to reduce sticking.*

# Green Goddess Burgers

*For after the game or show. Or maybe just a midnight snack!*

2 slices bacon
12 oz. ground beef
1 tablespoon milk
1/2 teaspoon salt
Dash pepper

1/2 (8-oz.) can spinach, drained and chopped
1 hard-boiled egg, chopped
1 tablespoon green goddess salad dressing
2 slices French bread, cut 1-inch thick

Prepare unit for open grilling. Cook bacon on preheated grill until crisp, about 3 minutes. Remove bacon and keep warm. Drain grill. In a medium bowl, mix ground beef, milk, salt and pepper. Shape into 4 thin patties. In a small bowl, mix spinach, egg and salad dressing. Spoon onto center of 2 patties. Cover with remaining patties. Seal edges with fingertips. Cook on grill until brown, 3 to 4 minutes on each side. Top each burger with a bacon slice. Serve open-face on French bread. Makes 2 open-face burgers.

# Lasagna Burgers

*This one will keep them coming back for more.*

8 oz. ground beef
1 egg, slightly beaten
4 teaspoons fine dry breadcrumbs
1/2 teaspoon dehydrated minced onion flakes
1/4 teaspoon salt
1/4 teaspoon Worcestershire sauce
1/8 teaspoon dried basil
Dash garlic salt

Dash pepper
2 tablespoons cottage cheese with chives
1 tablespoon grated Parmesan cheese
1/2 (8-oz.) can tomato sauce
Dash dried oregano
2 slices mozzarella cheese
2 hamburger rolls

Prepare unit for open grilling. In a medium bowl, mix beef, egg, breadcrumbs, onion flakes, salt, Worcestershire sauce, basil, garlic salt and pepper. Shape into 4 thin patties. Top 2 patties with 1 tablespoon cottage cheese each, spreading to within 1/2 inch of edge. Sprinkle each with 1-1/2 teaspoons Parmesan cheese. Cover with remaining patties. Seal edges with fingertips. Cook on preheated grill until brown, 3 to 4 minutes on each side. Remove and keep warm. Pour tomato sauce onto grill; stir in oregano. Cook and stir until heated through, about 1 minute. Spoon over patties; top with cheese slices. Serve on hamburger rolls. Makes 2 servings.

# *Chip & Dip Burgers*

*Substitute your own favorite dip for Cheddar cheese sour cream dip.*

8 oz. ground beef
1/4 cup crushed potato chips
1/4 cup Cheddar cheese sour cream dip
2 tablespoons pickle relish

2 hamburger rolls
1/4 cup Cheddar cheese sour cream dip
1/4 cup crushed potato chips

Prepare unit for closed grilling. In a medium bowl, mix beef, 1/4 cup potato chips, 1/4 cup sour cream dip and relish. Mix well. Shape into 2 patties. Place on preheated grill. Close lid; latch handle. Cook until brown, about 2-1/2 minutes on each side. Serve on hamburger rolls topped with remaining 1/4 cup sour cream dip and 1/4 cup crushed potato chips. Makes 2 burgers.

# *Sloppy Joes*

*Yummy Joes would be a better name!*

8 oz. ground beef
2 tablespoons chopped onion
2 tablespoons chopped green pepper
2 tablespoons chopped celery
1/4 teaspoon garlic salt

1/2 cup ketchup
1 teaspoon prepared mustard
1 teaspoon Worcestershire sauce
3 hamburger rolls

Prepare unit for open grilling. On preheated grill, combine beef, onion, green pepper, celery and garlic salt. Cook and stir until meat is brown and vegetables are tender, about 6-1/2 minutes. Stir in ketchup, mustard and Worcestershire sauce. Cook and stir until heated through, about 1-1/2 minutes. Serve on hamburger rolls. Makes 3 servings.

*Suggested seasonings for beef are: basil, chervil, garlic, marjoram, oregano, parsley, rosemary, tansy and thyme.*

# Bagel Burgers

*Horseradish and beef is hard to beat!*

8 oz. ground beef
2 tablespoons chopped dill pickle
1-1/2 teaspoons prepared horseradish
1/2 teaspoon dehydrated minced onion flakes

1/2 teaspoon salt
Dash pepper
2 bagels, split
1/2 (3-oz.) pkg. cream cheese, softened

Prepare unit for closed grilling. In a medium bowl, mix beef, pickle, horseradish, onion flakes, salt and pepper. Shape into 2 patties. Place on preheated grill. Close lid; latch handle. Cook until brown, about 2 minutes on each side. Spread bagels with cream cheese. Serve patties on bagels. Makes 2 burgers.

# Far East Burgers

*Serve on a dinner plate with rice and vegetables or on French bread.*

8 oz. ground beef
3 tablespoons finely chopped water chestnuts
1 tablespoon chopped green onion
2 tablespoons soy sauce

1 tablespoon dry white wine
1/2 teaspoon honey
1/2 clove garlic, minced
Dash ground ginger

In a medium bowl, mix beef, water chestnuts and onion. Shape into 2 patties. Place in a shallow dish. In a small bowl, mix soy sauce, wine, honey, garlic and ginger. Pour over patties. Refrigerate several hours; drain. Prepare unit for open grilling. Cook patties on preheated grill until brown, about 3 minutes on each side. Spoon juices over patties. Makes 2 servings.

# Hawaiian Honey Burgers

*A touch of Waikiki!*

8 oz. ground beef
1 tablespoon honey
Dash ground cinnamon
Dash curry powder

Dash ground ginger
2 slices pineapple
Soy sauce

Prepare unit for open grilling. In a medium bowl, mix beef, honey, cinnamon, curry powder and ginger. Shape into 2 patties. Cook on preheated grill until brown, about 3 minutes. Turn and top with pineapple slices. Brush with soy sauce. Cook until other side is brown, about another 3 minutes. Makes 2 servings.

# Beer & Onion Burgers

*Onions sautéed in beer garnish this juicy burger.*

8 oz. ground beef
1/4 cup beer
1 teaspoon seasoned salt
2 Kaiser rolls
2 tablespoons butter or margarine
1 small onion, sliced and separated into rings

1/4 cup beer
1 tablespoon steak sauce
1/4 teaspoon dried basil
1/4 teaspoon dried thyme
Lettuce and tomato slices, if desired

Prepare unit for closed grilling. In a medium bowl, mix beef, 1/4 cup beer and seasoned salt. Shape into 2 patties. Place on preheated grill. Close lid; latch handle. Cook until brown, about 2 minutes on each side. Place on rolls and keep warm. Prepare unit for open grilling. Melt butter or margarine on grill. Add onion. Cook and stir until tender, about 4 minutes. Stir in remaining 1/4 cup beer, steak sauce, basil and thyme. Cook and stir until heated through, about 2 minutes. Spoon onion mixture on top of patties. Serve with lettuce and tomato slices, if desired. Makes 2 servings.

# Herb-Butter Topping for Burgers

*Choose your favorite flavor.*

1/4 cup butter or margarine, softened
1 tablespoon snipped fresh parsley

1 tablespoon chopped green onion
1/2 teaspoon seasoned salt

In a small bowl, blend butter or margarine, parsley, onion and seasoned salt. Spread on hot grilled hamburgers just before serving. Or shape into a small roll and refrigerate. Slice when ready to use. Place 1 butter slice on each hot grilled hamburger before serving.

**Variations**
Add 2 tablespoons grated Parmesan cheese, *or* 1 tablespoon bottled steak sauce *or* 1/2 teaspoon dried dillweed to butter or margarine with parsley, onion and seasoned salt.

**Beer & Onion Burger**

# California Super Burgers

*West Coast style—quick, casual and delicious.*

8 oz. ground beef
1/4 cup dairy sour cream
1/2 (.56-oz.) pkg. onion-bacon dip mix

1 tablespoon fine dry breadcrumbs
2 hamburger rolls

Prepare unit for closed grilling. In a medium bowl, mix beef, sour cream, dip mix and breadcrumbs. Shape into 2 patties. Place on preheated grill. Close lid; latch handle. Cook until brown, about 2 minutes on each side. Serve on hamburger rolls. Makes 2 burgers.

# Curry Condiment Burgers

*Chutney makes an unusual topping for an exotic burger.*

2 tablespoons chopped salted peanuts
1 tablespoon flaked coconut
1 tablespoon raisins
12 oz. ground beef

1/2 teaspoon curry powder
2 hamburger rolls
Chutney

Prepare unit for closed grilling. In a small bowl, mix peanuts, coconut and raisins; set aside. In a medium bowl, combine beef and curry powder; mix well. Shape into 4 patties. Spoon peanut mixture onto 2 patties. Cover with remaining patties; seal edges with fingertips. Place on preheated grill. Close lid, but do not latch handle. Cook until brown, 3-1/2 to 4 minutes on each side. Serve on hamburger rolls topped with chutney. Makes 2 burgers.

# Tuna Burgers

*Serve with a salad or on hamburger rolls with pickle relish and hard-boiled egg slices.*

1/2 (7-1/4-oz.) can tuna, drained and flaked
1/2 cup soft breadcrumbs (1-1/2 slices bread)
1 egg, beaten
1-1/2 teaspoons ketchup

1/2 teaspoon dehydrated minced onion flakes
1/2 teaspoon sweet pickle relish
1/2 teaspoon lemon juice
1 tablespoon butter or margarine

Prepare unit for open grilling. In a medium bowl, mix tuna, breadcrumbs, egg, ketchup, onion flakes, pickle relish and lemon juice. Shape into 2 patties. On preheated grill, melt butter or margarine. Add patties and cook until brown, about 2 minutes on each side. Makes 2 patties.

# Mushroom Burgers Deluxe

*Whip up these bacon-mushroom stuffed burgers for unexpected guests.*

3 slices bacon
1/2 cup fresh mushroom slices
1/4 teaspoon garlic salt

12 oz. ground beef
2 hamburger rolls
Canned French-fried onions

Prepare unit for open grilling. Cook bacon on preheated grill until crisp, 3 to 4 minutes. Remove bacon, reserve drippings on grill. Crumble bacon and set aside. Add mushrooms and garlic salt to drippings. Cook and stir until mushrooms are barely tender, about 1/2 minutes. Add mushrooms to bacon. Shape beef into 4 patties. Spoon mushroom-bacon mixture onto 2 patties. Cover with remaining patties; seal edges with fingertips. Cook patties on grill until brown, about 5 minutes on each side. Serve on hamburger rolls topped with French-fried onions. Makes 2 burgers.

# Burgundy Burgers

*Toast your French bread on the grill before cooking the burgers.*

8 oz. ground beef
2 tablespoons Burgundy
Dash garlic salt
2 tablespoons butter or margarine

1/2 cup fresh mushroom slices
2 tablespoons chopped green onion
1/4 cup Burgundy
2 slices French bread

Prepare unit for closed grilling. In a medium bowl, mix beef, 2 tablespoons Burgundy and garlic salt. Shape into 2 patties. Place on preheated grill. Close lid; latch handle. Cook until brown, about 2 minutes on each side. Remove and keep warm. Prepare unit for open grilling. Melt butter or margarine on grill. Add mushrooms and onion. Cook and stir until tender, about 3 minutes. Stir in remaining 1/4 cup Burgundy. Cook and stir until heated through, about 1/2 minute. Serve patties on French bread topped with mushroom sauce. Makes 2 open-face burgers.

# Guacamole Burgers

*If you're in a hurry, substitute frozen guacamole dip for the avocado mixture.*

1 avocado, peeled, seeded and mashed
1 tablespoon chopped canned green chilies
1 teaspoon grated onion
1 tablespoon lemon juice
1/2 teaspoon garlic salt
8 oz. ground beef

1 small tomato, peeled and chopped
1/2 teaspoon garlic salt
1/2 teaspoon chili powder
2 slices French bread
Corn chips

Prepare unit for closed grilling. In a small bowl, combine avocado, chilies, onion, lemon juice and 1/2 teaspoon garlic salt. Mix well and chill. In a medium bowl, mix beef, tomato, 1/2 teaspoon garlic salt and chili powder. Shape into 2 patties. Place on preheated grill. Close lid; latch handle. Cook until brown, about 2 minutes on each side. Serve on French bread. Top with chilled avocado mixture and corn chips. Makes 2 open-face burgers.

# Sauerkraut Burgers

*A variation of the classic Reuben sandwich.*

8 oz. ground beef
2 tablespoons shredded Swiss cheese
1/2 teaspoon salt
Dash pepper
Vegetable oil

2 slices pumpernickel bread
1/4 cup sauerkraut, drained and rinsed
2 tablespoons finely chopped apple
1 tablespoon chopped green onion
1/2 teaspoon caraway seed

Prepare unit for closed grilling. In a medium bowl, mix beef, cheese, salt and pepper. Shape into 2 patties. Brush both sides of preheated grill with oil. Place patties on grill. Close lid; latch handle. Cook until brown, about 2 minutes on each side. Place patties on bread slices; keep warm. Combine sauerkraut, apple, onion and caraway seed on grill. Cook and stir until heated through, about 2 minutes. Spoon on top of patties. Makes 2 open-face burgers.

# Health Burgers

*Ham and pork burgers with a crunchy nutritious filling and a unique trio on top.*

4 oz. ground ham
4 oz. ground pork
2 tablespoons grated carrot
2 tablespoons raisins
1 tablespoon toasted sunflower seeds

Vegetable oil
2 whole-wheat hamburger rolls
Alfalfa sprouts
2 slices pineapple
Chutney

Prepare unit for open grilling. In a medium bowl, mix ham and pork. Shape into 4 thin patties. In a small bowl, mix carrot, raisins and sunflower seeds. Spoon onto centers of 2 patties. Cover with remaining patties; seal edges with fingertips. Brush oil on preheated grill. Cook patties on grill until brown, 3 to 4 minutes on each side. Place patties on rolls. Top with alfalfa sprouts, pineapple slices and chutney. Makes 2 burgers.

## How to Make Health Burgers

1/Spoon carrot-raisin filling on top of half the pork burgers. Top with a second burger and seal the edges with your fingertips.

2/Serve these tasty burgers on whole-wheat hamburger rolls topped with alfalfa sprouts, a pineapple ring and chutney.

# Porcupine Burgers

*Rice and beef topped with spicy tomato sauce make a complete meal.*

8 oz. ground beef
1/4 cup cooked rice
2 tablespoons chopped onion
1/2 (10-1/2-oz.) can condensed tomato soup
1/2 teaspoon dried basil

1 tablespoon Worcestershire sauce
1 teaspoon prepared mustard
2 hamburger rolls
Green pepper rings for garnish

Prepare unit for closed grilling. In a medium bowl, combine beef, rice, onion, 2 tablespoons of the condensed soup and basil; mix well. Shape into 2 patties. Place on preheated grill. Close lid; latch handle. Cook until brown, about 2 minutes on each side. Remove and keep warm. Prepare unit for open grilling. Combine remaining soup, Worcestershire sauce and mustard on grill. Cook and stir until heated through, about 1 minute. Serve patties on hamburger rolls topped with sauce. Garnish with green pepper rings. Makes 2 burgers.

# Sausage-Stuffed Pork Burgers

*Herb-seasoned stuffing and sausage lend a spicy flavor to this juicy burger.*

Vegetable oil
3 oz. bulk pork sausage
1 tablespoon chopped onion
1 tablespoon chopped celery
3 tablespoons herb-seasoned breadcrumbs
   for stuffing

8 oz. ground pork
2 hamburger rolls
Cranberry-orange relish

Prepare unit for open grilling. Brush preheated grill with oil. Cook sausage, onion and celery in oil, stirring often, until meat is brown and vegetables are tender, about 4-1/2 minutes. Place sausage mixture in bowl; toss with stuffing. Moisten with a little water if necessary. Shape ground pork into 4 thin patties. Spoon stuffing mixture onto 2 patties. Cover with remaining patties. Seal edges with fingertips. Cook patties on grill until brown, about 5-1/2 minutes on each side. Serve on hamburger rolls topped with cranberry-orange relish. Makes 2 burgers.

---

*Burgers filled with a tasty stuffing are a pleasant surprise. To seal stuffed burgers, press edges firmly together with fingertips around entire burger. Be sure no stuffing is spilling out along edges.*

# Greek Isle Burgers

*Yogurt and mint add a Mediterranean touch to lamb burgers.*

1/4 cup chopped, peeled cucumber
2 tablespoons chopped green onion
1/2 teaspoon dried mint
1 teaspoon vegetable oil
12 oz. ground lamb
3 tablespoons plain yogurt

Garlic salt
2 Kaiser rolls
Crisp lettuce leaves
1 tomato, sliced
Crumbled feta cheese
Dried oregano

Prepare unit for closed grilling. In a small bowl, mix cucumber, onion, mint and oil; set aside. In a medium bowl, mix lamb and yogurt. Shape into 4 thin patties. Sprinkle with garlic salt. Spoon cucumber mixture onto center of 2 patties. Cover with remaining patties. Seal edges with fingertips. Place patties on preheated grill. Close lid; latch handle. Cook until brown, about 4 minutes on each side for medium. Place on Kaiser rolls. Top with lettuce leaves, tomato slices and feta cheese. Sprinkle with oregano. Makes 2 burgers.

# Chicken Burgers

*After Thanksgiving, substitute turkey for the chicken.*

1 cup ground cooked chicken
1 egg, slightly beaten
2 tablespoons mayonnaise
1 tablespoon pickle relish
1/2 teaspoon salt

Dash pepper
Vegetable oil
2 hamburger rolls
Sliced pickles *or* cranberry sauce

Prepare unit for open grilling. In a medium bowl, mix chicken, egg, mayonnaise, pickle relish, salt and pepper. Shape into 2 patties. Brush preheated grill with oil. Cook patties in oil until brown, about 2 minutes on each side. Serve on hamburger rolls with sliced pickles or cranberry sauce. Makes 2 burgers.

# Hot Dog!

If you're grilling plain hot dogs, let yourself go! Add some adventurous toppings. Try chopped onion and green pepper, chopped tomatoes, shredded cheese, chopped pickles, cole slaw or sauerkraut, mustard, ketchup, horseradish and whatever else you have on hand. Line them up like a buffet or mix them in a sauce. Hot dogs are always delicious, but with sauce or relishes they can be more flavorful and satisfying than a 4 course dinner!

Friends and family will hurry back for seconds when you fix Chili Dogs or Tangy Barbecued Franks. Announce ahead of time that you're serving Mexican Dogs or Frankly Hot Three Bean Salad and there won't be enough room at the table to seat everybody.

Ball games and hot dogs are a natural pair but Pizza Burger Dogs and Bratwurst & Sauerkraut are 2 frankfurters you can't buy at the ball park. Take your own along, or settle down with the TV and enjoy them at home.

# *Frankfurter Favorites*

*A good basic hot dog recipe. Fabulous, different hot dogs are in the variations.*

**4 frankfurters**
**4 hot dog rolls**

Prepare unit for closed grilling. Place frankfurters on preheated grill. Close lid; latch handle. Cook until heated through, about 2 minutes on each side. Remove and place on hot dog rolls. Makes 4 servings.

**Variations**

**Vegetable Dogs:** Top each frank with chopped tomato, chopped onion, chopped green or red pepper, chopped pimiento, sliced cucumber and pepperoncini (pickled hot Italian peppers).
**Onion Dogs:** Prepare unit for open grilling. Slice 1 onion and separate into rings. Add 2 tablespoons oil to preheated grill. Cook onion in oil until tender, about 4 minutes. Place on top of franks.
**Cheese Dogs:** Top each frank with 2 tablespoons shredded process American cheese.

# *Sausage & Egg Sandwich*

*Try this one for breakfast, lunch or dinner.*

| | |
|---|---|
| **2 tablespoons butter or margarine, softened** | **1 tablespoon vegetable oil** |
| **2 teaspoons prepared mustard** | **2 eggs** |
| **2 slices bread** | **2 slices American cheese** |
| **1 smoked link sausage, halved** | **Relish or green pepper, if desired** |

Prepare unit for closed grilling. In a small bowl, place butter or margarine and mustard. Beat to blend well. Spread on bread slices. Split sausage halves lengthwise, cutting to other side, but not through. Open and place on preheated grill. Close lid; latch handle. Cook until heated through, about 3 minutes on each side  Place sausage on bread slices and keep warm. Prepare unit for open grilling. Add oil to preheated grill. Break eggs onto grill. Cook until set, about 1 minute. Turn and cook until done, about 1 minute for over-easy. Place each egg on top of a sausage half. Top with cheese slices. Serve with relish or green pepper, if desired. Makes 2 open-face servings.

> *Add a special touch to hot dogs with homemade relish. Combine 1/4 cup finely chopped onion, 1/4 cup finely chopped pickle and 4 teaspoons prepared mustard; mix well. Makes about 1/2 cup relish.*

# Pizza Burger Dogs

*Old favorites get together with new appeal.*

1 egg, slightly beaten
3/4 cup soft breadcrumbs (2-1/4 slices bread)
1/4 cup milk
1 teaspoon chili powder
1/2 teaspoon salt
1/2 teaspoon dried oregano
1/2 teaspoon cumin

1 lb. ground beef
6 frankfurters
2 tablespoons vegetable oil
6 hot dog rolls
1 (8-oz.) can pizza sauce
Grated Parmesan cheese

Prepare unit for open grilling. In a large bowl, mix egg, bread crumbs, milk, chili powder, salt, oregano and cumin. Add beef; mix thoroughly. Divide into 6 portions. Shape each portion around a frankfurter. Add oil to preheated grill. Cook burger dogs, 3 at a time, until done, about 6 minutes, turning several times to cook all sides. Place on hot dog rolls and keep warm. Repeat with remaining burger dogs. Drain drippings from grill. Add pizza sauce to grill. Cook and stir until hot, about 3-1/2 minutes. Spoon over burger dogs and sprinkle with Parmesan cheese. Makes 6 servings.

## How to Make Pizza Burger Dogs

1/Divide the ground beef mixture into 6 equal portions. Shape each portion into a long oval patty, then mold the patty around the dog. If the beef mixture is too soft to handle, chill the mixture for a few hours.

2/Cook the burger dogs in 2 batches. Use 2 wooden spoons or spatulas to turn them often so they will cook evenly on all sides. Wrap the first 3 cooked burger dogs in foil to keep warm while the last 3 are cooking.

# Chili Dogs

*Whip up your old favorite in a jiffy.*

4 frankfurters
4 hot dog rolls

1 (10-oz.) can chili
1/2 cup shredded Cheddar cheese (2 oz.)

Prepare unit for closed grilling. Place frankfurters on preheated grill. Close lid; latch handle. Cook until heated through, about 2 minutes on each side. Remove and place on hot dog rolls; keep warm. Prepare unit for open grilling. Pour chili onto grill. Cook and stir until heated through, about 2 minutes. Spoon onto frankfurters and top with cheese. Makes 4 servings.

# Mexican Dogs

*Teenagers' delight!*

3 frankfurters
2 oz. Monterey Jack cheese
1/2 canned green chili pepper

3 tortillas
Vegetable oil
Taco sauce or ketchup, if desired

Prepare unit for closed grilling. Cut lengthwise splits in frankfurters, cutting to other side, but not through. Cut cheese into 3 strips; insert into split frankfurters. Cut chili pepper into 3 strips; place on cheese. Wrap a tortilla around each stuffed frankfurter. Brush rolled tortillas with oil. Place on preheated grill. Close lid, but do not latch. Cook until heated through, about 1-1/2 minutes on each side. Serve with taco sauce or ketchup, if desired. Makes 3 servings.

# Spanish Dogs

*Don't let the chili peppers scare you. Use as few as you want.*

4 frankfurters, cut in 1-inch pieces
1/2 (15-1/2-oz.) can refried beans (1 cup)
1/2 cup process American cheese,
   cut in 1/2-inch cubes (2-oz.)
2 to 4 canned green chili peppers, chopped

4 hot dog rolls
Shredded lettuce
Chopped tomatoes
Taco sauce

Prepare unit for open grilling. Cook frankfurter pieces on preheated grill until heated through, about 3 minutes, turning occasionally. Remove and keep warm. Add beans to grill. Cook and stir until heated through, about 2 minutes. Stir in frankfurter pieces, cheese and chili peppers. Spoon onto hot dog rolls. Top with lettuce, tomatoes and taco sauce. Makes 4 servings.

# Frankly Hot Three Bean Salad

*Use jumbo frankfurters for man-size appetites.*

3 slices bacon
1/4 cup chopped onion
1 (8-oz.) can kidney beans, drained
1 (8-oz.) can wax beans, drained

1 (8-oz.) can green beans, drained
1/4 cup French dressing with spices and herbs
2 tablespoons chopped pimiento
4 frankfurters

Prepare unit for open grilling. Cook bacon on preheated grill until crisp, 3 to 4 minutes. Remove bacon; reserve drippings on grill. Crumble bacon and set aside. Add onion to bacon drippings on grill. Cook and stir until tender, about 1-1/2 minutes. Stir in beans, dressing and pimiento. Cook and stir until heated through, about 2-1/2 minutes. Remove bean salad and keep warm. Score frankfurters diagonally at 1/2-inch intervals. Place in bowl of hot water for 30 seconds. Remove from water and place on preheated grill. Cook and turn until frankfurters curl and are heated through, about 2 minutes. Spoon hot bean salad inside frank corkscrews. Top with crumbled bacon. Makes 4 servings.

# Italian Sausage Sandwich

*This hearty sandwich is a favorite at Italian street fairs.*

2 tablespoons vegetable oil
8 oz. Italian sausage,
   cut in 1-inch pieces
1/4 cup chopped onion
1/4 cup chopped green pepper

1 clove garlic, minced
1-1/4 cups Italian cooking sauce
2 teaspoons sugar
1 teaspoon chili powder
2 submarine rolls

Prepare unit for open grilling. Add oil to preheated grill. Place sausage, onion, green pepper and garlic on grill. Cook and stir until sausage is done, 3 to 4 minutes. In a small bowl, mix Italian cooking sauce, sugar and chili powder. Add to sausage mixture. Cook and stir until heated through, about 1 minute. Serve on submarine rolls. Makes 2 servings.

# Cheese & Bacon Wrap-Ups

*A hot dog stuffed with cheese and wrapped in crisp bacon. Mmmm.*

4 frankfurters
1 slice process American cheese,
   cut in 1-inch strips
4 slices bacon

4 hot dog rolls
Mustard, if desired
Ketchup, if desired

Prepare unit for open grilling. Cut frankfurters in half lengthwise. Place cheese strips on bottom halves of frankfurters and cover with top halves. Wrap each with 1 slice of bacon; secure with wooden picks. Cook on preheated grill until bacon is done and frank is heated through, 6 to 8 minutes, turning several times. Serve on hot dog rolls. Top with mustard and catsup, if desired. Makes 4 servings.

# Tangy Barbecued Franks

*Enjoy the great taste of barbecuing all year long.*

4 frankfurters
1 (8-oz.) can tomato sauce
1/4 cup brown sugar, firmly packed
1 tablespoon Worcestershire sauce

1 tablespoon prepared mustard
1/4 teaspoon bottled hot pepper sauce
4 hot dog rolls

Prepare unit for closed grilling. Place frankfurters on preheated grill. Close lid; latch handle. Cook until heated through, about 2 minutes on each side. In a small bowl, mix tomato sauce, brown sugar, Worcestershire sauce, mustard and hot pepper sauce. Prepare unit for open grilling. Place hot frankfurters on grill. Pour sauce over frankfurters. Cook and stir until sauce is heated through, about 3 minutes. Serve on hot dog rolls. Makes 4 servings.

---

*Frankfurters are widely available in various sizes. The timings in this book are based on 10 frankfurters per pound. If you use larger or smaller franks, you may need to adjust the timing slightly.*

# Idaho Favorite

*Try this out on your meat-and-potato enthusiasts!*

1 cup water
2/3 cup instant mashed potato flakes
1/2 cup shredded Cheddar cheese
1/4 cup dairy sour cream

2 tablespoons dried chives
6 frankfurters
6 hot dog rolls

Prepare unit for open grilling. Add water to preheated grill. Bring to a boil, 1-1/2 to 2 minutes. In a small bowl, mix potato flakes, cheese, sour cream and chives. Pour boiling water over potato mixture; mix well. Cut lengthwise slits in frankfurters, cutting to other side, but not through. Fill slits with potato mixture. Place frankfurters on grill. Cook until heated through, about 6 minutes, turning to cook all sides. Serve on hot dog rolls. Makes 6 servings.

# Inside-Out Corn Dogs

*Enjoy the good, satisfying taste of corn dogs without deep-frying.*

4 oz. bulk pork sausage
1 tablespoon chopped celery
1 tablespoon chopped onion
1 cup corn bread stuffing mix
Water
4 jumbo frankfurters

1 (8-oz.) can tomatoes, drained and mashed
2 tablespoons chopped onion
2 tablespoons canned chopped green chilies
1 clove garlic, minced
4 hot dog rolls

Prepare unit for open grilling. Cook sausage, celery and 1 tablespoon onion on preheated grill until sausage is done and vegetables are tender, about 3-1/2 minutes. Place in a large bowl; reserve drippings on grill. Add stuffing mix and seasoning packet to sausage mixture. Reduce water specified on stuffing mix directions by 1/2 cup. Add to stuffing mixture and mix well. Cut lengthwise slits in frankfurters, cutting to other side, but not through. Fill slits with stuffing mixture; set aside. Add tomatoes, 2 tablespoons onion, chilies and garlic to sausage drippings on grill. Cook and stir until heated through, 2 to 3 minutes. Place tomato sauce in a serving bowl; set aside. Place stuffed frankfurters on grill. Cook until heated through, about 3 minutes, turning to cook all sides. Serve on hot dog rolls with tomato sauce. Makes 4 servings.

# Polynesian Stuffed Bratwurst

*A zingy-flavored dish to brighten your next luncheon.*

4 smoked bratwurst

2 tablespoons prepared mustard

1 (8-oz.) can pineapple chunks, drained

4 slices bacon

4 hot dog rolls

Prepare unit for open grilling. Cut lengthwise slits in bratwurst, cutting to other side, but not through. Spread inside of slits with mustard. Cut pineapple chunks in half and place in slits. Wrap bacon around bratwurst, securing with wooden picks. Cook on preheated grill until bacon is done and bratwurst is heated through, turning several times, 6 to 8 minutes. Serve on hot dog rolls. Makes 4 servings.

## How to Make Polynesian Stuffed Bratwurst

1/Split smoked bratwurst lengthwise, cutting to, but not through, the other side of the bratwurst. Spread the inside of the slit with as much mustard as you'd like. Stuff the slits with pineapple chunks.

2/Wind a strip of bacon around each bratwurst. Insert toothpicks *diagonally* through the bacon and bratwurst to hold the bacon in place. Toothpicks inserted crosswise make poor use of the grill space.

# Bratwurst & Sauerkraut

*A German favorite!*

2 smoked bratwurst, cut in 1-inch pieces
1 (8-oz.) can sauerkraut, drained and
  rinsed

1/2 cup chopped green onion
1 teaspoon caraway seed
2 onion rolls

Prepare unit for open grilling. Cook bratwurst on preheated grill until heated through, about 3 minutes, turning to cook on all sides. Stir in sauerkraut, onions and caraway seed. Cook and stir until heated through, about 2 minutes. Serve on onion rolls. Makes 2 servings.

# Rhinelander Sandwich

*A robust sandwich! Dill pickles, potato chips and beer add the final touch.*

2 knockwurst or smoked bratwurst
2 oz. Monterey Jack or Muenster cheese
4 slices rye or pumpernickel bread

Dijon-style or spicy brown mustard
2 tablespoons chopped green onion

Prepare unit for closed grilling. Place sausage on preheated grill. Close lid; latch handle. Cook until heated through, about 3 minutes on each side. Remove and cut in half lengthwise. Slice cheese about 1/8-inch thick. Spread 1 side of each bread slice with mustard. Top 2 of the bread slices with cheese, onion and sausage halves. Cover with remaining bread slices. Place sandwiches on grill; close lid, but do not latch. Cook until toasted, about 1 minute on each side. Makes 2 sandwiches.

# Sandwiches

Not by bread alone—and that's what these sandwiches are all about. But be sure to take advantage of the variety of breads available in your supermarket. There's everything from sprout bread to whole-grain bread and gourmet breads from all over the world. Athenian-Style Lamb & Pita is different but delicious.

If you plan to grill a many-layered dagwood, you'll have a better sandwich if you use the open-grilling technique and turn the sandwich over to brown both sides. For thinner sandwiches, closed grilling works fine—and it's faster.

Hot sandwiches can turn leftover roast, ham or turkey into something special. You can even use more than 1 leftover in Turkey-Berry Sandwiches. You'll find some fabulous variations of old standbys like Deluxe BLTs and Italian Meatball Submarines in this section too.

If you like fish sandwiches, you'll be ecstatic over breaded fish sticks and fish portions on toasted buns, covered with a flavorful sauce. Go a step further and try Curried Fish Sandwiches.

See what you can do to improve on Vegetarian Delight. With all the crisp vegetables, bean sprouts and nut butters available, no sandwich has to be the same!

# Steak & Cheese Subs

*Thinly sliced sirloin tip is often labeled* breakfast steak *and is usually an economical buy.*

3 tablespoons butter or margarine
1 onion, sliced and separated into rings
2 (3-oz.) thinly sliced sirloin tip steaks
Garlic salt
Pepper

2 slices Cheddar cheese
2 submarine rolls
Crisp lettuce leaves
4 or more slices tomato
Horseradish sauce

Prepare unit for open grilling. Melt butter or margarine on preheated grill. Cook and stir onion slices in butter or margarine until tender, about 4 minutes. Remove and keep warm. Drain grill. Sprinkle sirloin tip slices with garlic salt and pepper. Cook 1 at a time until brown, about 1 minute. Turn and top with cheese slices. Cook until done, about 1 minute for rare. Place on submarine rolls. Top with grilled onions, lettuce leaves and tomato slices. Spread with horseradish sauce. Makes 2 submarine sandwiches.

# Hearty Roast Beef Sandwiches

*Sunday's pot roast tastes even better on Monday with this creamy sauce.*

Cream Sauce, see below
2 slices white bread
2 tablespoons butter or margarine
2 slices cooked roast beef
1 tablespoon butter or margarine

1 tablespoon all-purpose flour
1/2 cup beef broth
1 teaspoon Worcestershire sauce
Salt and pepper to taste

*Cream Sauce:*
2 tablespoons dairy sour cream
1 teaspoon Dijon-style mustard

Prepare Cream Sauce; set aside. Prepare unit for open grilling. Lightly toast bread on preheated grill, about 1 minute. Turn and lightly toast other side, about 1 minute. Remove and keep warm. Melt 2 tablespoons butter or margarine on grill. Cook and turn roast beef in butter or margarine until heated through, about 2 minutes. Place on toasted bread and keep warm. Melt 1 tablespoon butter or margarine on grill. Stir in flour. In a small bowl, mix beef broth and Worcestershire sauce; stir into flour mixture. Cook and stir until thickened, about 2 minutes. Season to taste with salt and pepper. Spoon over roast beef and bread. Top with dollop of Cream Sauce. Makes 2 open-face sandwiches.

Cream Sauce:
In a small bowl, mix sour cream and mustard. Makes about 2-1/2 tablespoons topping.

# Grilled Beefwiches

*This energy-packed lunch uses leftover beef.*

2 tablespoons dry onion-soup mix
1 tablespoon water
1 teaspoon prepared horseradish
Dash pepper

3 tablespoons butter or margarine, softened
4 slices white bread
4 thin slices cooked roast beef or corned beef
2 slices process cheese

Prepare unit for open grilling. Soften soup mix in water. In a small bowl, mix soup mix, horseradish and pepper. Stir into butter or margarine; mix well. Spread on 1 side of each bread slice. Top buttered side of 2 bread slices with 2 slices beef and 1 slice cheese. Cover with second bread slice. Cook sandwiches on preheated grill until toasted, about 1 minute on each side. Makes 2 sandwiches.

# Confetti Smoked Beef

*An appetizing sandwich for a cold winter day. Serve with a green salad.*

2 slices white bread
1 tablespoon butter or margarine, softened
1 (3-oz.) pkg. sliced smoked beef
2 tablespoons butter or margarine
2 tablespoons all-purpose flour

1 cup milk
2 tablespoons chopped pimiento
2 teaspoons dried parsley
Dash pepper

Prepare unit for open grilling. Spread bread slices with 1 tablespoon butter or margarine. Place on preheated grill. Cook until golden brown, about 1 minute on each side. Remove and keep warm. Tear beef into bite-size pieces. Melt 2 tablespoons butter or margarine on grill. Cook and turn beef in butter or margarine until heated through, about 2 minutes. Stir in flour. Add milk, pimiento, parsley and pepper. Cook and stir until thickened, about 2 minutes. Serve over toasted bread slices. Makes 2 open-face sandwiches.

---

*Suggested seasonings for fish are: anise, basil, chervil, cress, dill, fennel, garlic, lemon balm, marjoram, oregano, parsley, rosemary, savory, tansy, tarragon and thyme.*

# Deviled Ham, Egg & Cheese Sandwiches

*Here's a grilled sandwich that's both hearty and elegant.*

1 (3-oz.) pkg. cream cheese, softened
1 tablespoon milk
1/4 teaspoon dry mustard
1/8 teaspoon seasoned salt
1 (2-1/4-oz.) can deviled ham

3 hard-boiled eggs, chopped
1 tablespoon chopped green onion
8 slices bread
Vegetable oil

Prepare unit for open grilling. In a small bowl, beat cream cheese, milk, mustard and seasoned salt with electric mixer on medium speed until smooth. Stir in ham, eggs and onion. Spread on 4 bread slices. Cover with remaining bread slices. Brush preheated grill with oil. Cook sandwiches, 2 at a time, on grill until toasted, about 1 minute on each side. Makes 4 sandwiches.

# Croque-Monsieur Ham & Cheese Sandwiches

*My version of the ever-popular ham and cheese.*

1/2 cup finely grated Swiss cheese
2 tablespoons light cream
1/8 teaspoon salt
Dash pepper
4 slices bread

2 large slices cooked ham
1 egg
2 tablespoons light cream
Vegetable oil

Prepare unit for closed grilling. In a small bowl, mix cheese with 2 tablespoons cream to make a thick paste. Add salt and pepper. Cut crusts off bread slices. Spread 1 side of each bread slice with cheese mixture. Top 2 bread slices with ham. Cover with remaining bread slices, cheese side down. Press together firmly. Beat egg with 2 tablespoons cream. Dip each sandwich into egg mixture, letting bread soak up egg. Brush preheated grill with oil. Place sandwiches on grill. Close lid, but do not latch. Cook until golden brown, 1 to 2 minutes. Turn; brush grill again with oil. Cook until other side is golden brown, another 1 to 2 minutes. Makes 2 sandwiches.

# Athenian-Style Lamb & Pita

*If all the ingredients aren't in your supermarket, check local delicatessens and specialty stores.*

Cucumber-Garlic Sauce, see below
1 tablespoon vegetable oil
12 oz. lamb, cut in 1/2-inch cubes
2 tablespoons chopped onion
2 tablespoons chopped green pepper
1/2 teaspoon dried oregano, crushed

1/2 teaspoon garlic salt
2 to 4 pita breads, halved
Chopped tomato
Ripe olive slices
Crumbled feta cheese
Oregano, if desired

*Cucumber-Garlic Sauce:*
1 cup plain yogurt
1 medium cucumber, grated

1 teaspoon garlic salt

Prepare Cucumber-Garlic Sauce; set aside. Prepare unit for open grilling. Add oil to preheated grill. Add lamb cubes, onion, green pepper, oregano and garlic salt to oil. Cook and stir until lamb is done, about 4 minutes. Spoon lamb mixture into pita bread. Top with tomato, olives, cheese, Cucumber-Garlic Sauce and additional oregano, if desired. Makes 2 to 4 servings.

Cucumber-Garlic Sauce:
In a small bowl, mix yogurt, cucumber and garlic salt. Makes 1-1/2 cups.

# Reuben Sandwiches

*Ever-popular hot sandwiches you can make in a jiffy.*

4 slices rye bread
2 tablespoons Thousand Island dressing
4 slices cooked corned beef

2 slices Swiss cheese
4 tablespoons sauerkraut, drained and rinsed

Prepare unit for closed grilling. Spread 2 bread slices with dressing. Top with corned beef, cheese and sauerkraut. Cover with remaining bread slices. Place sandwiches on preheated grill. Close lid, but do not latch. Cook until toasted, 1 to 1-1/2 minutes on each side. Makes 2 sandwiches.

Athenian-Style Lamb & Pita

# Luau Sandwiches

*Pineapple and coconut make an irresistible sandwich.*

2 tablespoons vegetable oil
1 (12-oz.) can luncheon meat, sliced
   1/4-inch thick
4 slices whole-wheat bread

1 (8-oz.) can pineapple slices
2 tablespoons honey
2 tablespoons flaked coconut
4 maraschino cherries, if desired

Prepare unit for open grilling. Add oil to preheated grill. Cook luncheon meat slices 4 at a time until light brown, 1 to 2 minutes on each side. Place on bread slices and keep warm. Drain pineapple; reserve syrup. Grill pineapple slices until heated through, about 1 minute on each side. Place on top of luncheon meat on bread slices. In a small bowl, mix reserved pineapple syrup and honey. Pour onto grill. Cook and stir until heated through, 1 to 1-1/2 minutes. Spoon over pineapple slices and luncheon meat on bread slices. Sprinkle with coconut; top with maraschino cherries, if desired. Makes 4 open-face sandwiches.

# Deluxe BLTs

*Always appealing—even more so with Cheddar cheese and horseradish sauce.*

4 slices white bread
2 slices sharp Cheddar cheese
2 tablespoons horseradish sauce

4 slices bacon
Crisp lettuce leaves
1 tomato, sliced

Prepare unit for open grilling. Cook bread, 2 slices at a time, on preheated grill until lightly toasted, about 1 minute on each side. Top 2 bread slices with cheese. Spread remaining 2 bread slices with horseradish sauce; keep warm. Cook bacon on grill until crisp, 4 to 5 minutes, turning often. Place lettuce leaves on toasted bread spread with horseradish sauce. Top with bacon and tomato slices. Cover with remaining bread slices, cheese side down. Makes 2 sandwiches.

---

*Just about any type of luncheon meat can be grilled on the mini-grill for a sandwich or to serve plain. Melt a small amount of butter or margarine on the grill; cook meat until light brown and heated through, turning once.*

# Crunchy Ham Sandwiches

*Crunchy outside with a complete meal inside!*

4 slices white bread
1 tablespoon butter or margarine, softened
1 tablespoon prepared mustard
2 slices cooked ham
2 slices process American cheese
4 thin slices tomato

1 egg, slightly beaten
1 tablespoon milk
Dash onion salt
3/4 cup crushed corn chips or potato chips
2 tablespoons vegetable oil

Prepare unit for open grilling. Spread 2 bread slices on 1 side with butter or margarine. Spread remaining 2 bread slices on 1 side with mustard. Top each mustard-spread slice with 1 slice ham, 1 slice cheese and 2 slices tomato. Cover with slice of buttered bread, buttered side down. In a pie plate, mix egg, milk and onion salt. Dip sandwiches in egg mixture, then in crushed corn chips. Pat to secure chips to bread, turning to coat both sides. Add oil to preheated grill. Cook sandwiches in oil until golden brown, about 1 minute on each side. Makes 2 sandwiches.

## How to Make Crunchy Ham Sandwich

1/Spread bread slices with mustard, then layer with ham, cheese and tomato slices. Cover with a bread slice. Beat egg, milk and onion salt in a pie plate. Dip sandwich in the egg mixture.

2/Crush corn chips into another pie plate. Dip the egg-coated sandwiches in the corn chips, patting the chips gently to make them stick to the bread.

# Hot Club Sandwiches

*Star this for your next luncheon for two.*

3 slices bacon
2 English muffins, split
1 cup cubed cooked chicken
2 tablespoons chopped celery
2 tablespoons chopped pimiento

Salt and pepper to taste
1/2 cup plain yogurt
2 tablespoons mayonnaise
2 slices tomato
1 avocado, peeled, seeded and sliced

Prepare unit for open grilling. Cook bacon on preheated grill until crisp, 3 to 4 minutes. Drain bacon; reserve 3 tablespoons drippings in a small bowl. Crumble bacon and set aside. Pour 1 tablespoon bacon drippings onto grill. Toast 2 muffin halves, cut side down, about 1-1/2 minutes. Place on serving plates. Toast other muffin halves in another tablespoon bacon drippings. Cook and stir chicken, celery and pimiento in remaining 1 tablespoon bacon drippings on grill until heated through, about 3 minutes. Season to taste with salt and pepper. In a small bowl, mix yogurt and mayonnaise. Spoon half the yogurt mixture into the chicken mixture. Cook and stir until heated through, about 1 minute. Spoon chicken mixture onto 2 of the muffins. Cover with remaining muffins. Top with tomato and avocado slices. Spoon a dollop or remaining yogurt mixture on top. Sprinkle with crumbled bacon. Makes 2 sandwiches.

# Swiss Tenderloin Sandwiches

*A delightful texture with a choice blending of flavors.*

1 egg
1 tablespoon water
2 pork tenderloins, flattened into rounds
1 cup sesame-cheese cracker crumbs
1 tablespoon vegetable oil

1 slice Swiss cheese, halved diagonally
2 onion rolls, split
2 crisp lettuce leaves
2 tomato slices
Thousand Island dressing

Prepare unit for open grilling. In a pie plate, beat egg and water with a fork. Place cracker crumbs in another pie plate. Dip tenderloins in crumbs, then in egg, then back in crumbs. Add oil to preheated grill. Cook tenderloins until brown, about 5 minutes. Turn tenderloins. Place cheese halves on tenderloins. Cook until other side is brown and done, about another 5 minutes. Place on bottom half of onion rolls. Top with lettuce, tomato and Thousand Island dressing. Cover with top halves of rolls. Makes 2 sandwiches.

**Hot Club Sandwich**

# Grilled Pizza Sandwiches

*Pizza fans adore these sandwiches.*

4 slices bread
2 slices mozzarella cheese
4 thin slices tomato
1/2 (2-oz.) can anchovy fillets, drained

1 oz. thinly sliced pepperoni
Dried oregano to taste
Pepper to taste
2 tablespoons butter or margarine, softened

Prepare unit for open grilling. Top 2 bread slices with cheese, tomato, anchovies and pepperoni. Sprinkle with oregano and pepper. Cover with remaining bread slices. Spread both sides of sandwiches with butter or margarine. Cook on preheated grill until golden brown, about 1 minute on each side. Makes 2 sandwiches.

# Italian Meatball Submarines

*A delicious and economical addition to your menus.*

8 oz. bulk pork sausage
2 submarine rolls
1/4 cup chopped onion

1/4 cup chopped green pepper
3/4 cup Italian cooking sauce
1/2 cup shredded mozzarella cheese

Prepare unit for open grilling. Shape sausage into 1-inch balls. Cook sausage balls on preheated grill until done, about 5 minutes, turning often. Place on submarine rolls and keep warm; reserve sausage drippings on grill. Cook and stir onion and green pepper in sausage drippings until tender, about 2 minutes. Drain drippings. Add Italian cooking sauce to onion and green pepper on grill. Cook and stir until heated through, about 1 minute. Spoon sauce over meatballs on submarine rolls. Sprinkle with mozzarella cheese. Makes 2 submarine sandwiches.

---

*Suggested seasonings for pork are: caraway, coriander, fennel, garlic, oregano, parsley, sage, tansy and thyme.*

---

# Neptune's Delight

*A great catch in taste, economy and nutrition!*

2 tablespoons vegetable oil
1 (8-oz.) pkg. frozen breaded fish fillets
3 sesame seed hamburger rolls
1/4 cup mayonnaise

2 tablespoons chopped dill pickle
1 tablespoon chopped green olives
1 tablespoon lemon juice
1 hard-boiled egg, sliced

Prepare unit for open grilling. Add oil to preheated grill. Cook fish until brown, about 2-1/2 minutes on each side, or until fish flakes easily with a fork. Place fish on rolls. In a small bowl, mix mayonnaise, pickle, olives and lemon juice. Top fish with mayonnaise mixture and hard-boiled egg slices. Makes 3 sandwiches.

# Curried Fish Sandwiches

*Especially good served for brunch with fresh fruits.*

2 English muffins, split
2 tablespoons butter or margarine, softened
4 tablespoons vegetable oil
8 frozen breaded fish sticks
1 tablespoon butter or margarine
1 tablespoon all-purpose flour
1/4 teaspoon salt

1/4 teaspoon curry powder
1/4 teaspoon dry mustard
Dash pepper
2/3 cup milk
1/4 teaspoon dehydrated minced onion flakes
1 hard-boiled egg, chopped
2 tablespoons raisins

Prepare unit for open grilling. Spread split side of muffins with 2 tablespoons butter or margarine. Cook muffins, 2 halves at a time, buttered side up, on preheated grill until hot, 1 to 1-1/2 minutes. Remove and keep warm. Add 2 tablespoons oil to grill. Cook fish sticks, 4 at a time, in hot oil until brown, about 2 minutes on each side. Place fish sticks on muffin halves and keep warm. Repeat with remaining oil, fish sticks and muffin halves. Drain grill. Melt 1 tablespoon butter or margarine on grill. Blend in flour, salt, curry powder, mustard and pepper. Add milk and onion. Cook and stir until mixture thickens, 1 to 2 minutes. Stir in hard-boiled eggs. Spoon over fish sticks and sprinkle with raisins. Makes 4 open-face sandwiches.

# Turkey-Berry Sandwiches

*If you have whole-cranberry sauce left after the holidays, use it in place of jellied cranberry sauce.*

| | |
|---|---|
| 1/2 cup finely chopped cooked turkey or chicken | 4 teaspoons mayonnaise |
| 1 tablespoon chopped walnuts | 4 slices bread |
| 1 tablespoon finely chopped celery | 2 slices jellied cranberry sauce |
| | 2 tablespoons butter or margarine, softened |

Prepare unit for open grilling. In a small bowl, mix turkey, walnuts, celery and mayonnaise. Spread on 2 bread slices. Arrange cranberry slices on top of filling. Cover with remaining bread slices. Spread outside of bread slices with butter or margarine. Cook on preheated grill until golden brown, about 1 minute on each side. Makes 2 sandwiches.

# Monte Cristo Sandwiches

*A memorable lunch or Sunday night supper.*

| | |
|---|---|
| 4 slices bread | 1/2 cup milk |
| 2 slices Cheddar or Swiss cheese | 1/8 teaspoon salt |
| 2 large slices ham | Dash pepper |
| 2 slices salami or turkey | Vegetable oil |
| 1 egg | |

Prepare unit for closed grilling. Top 2 bread slices with cheese, ham and salami or turkey. Cover with remaining bread slices. In a pie plate, beat egg, milk, salt and pepper with a fork. Dip sandwiches in egg mixture, coating both sides. Brush preheated grill with oil. Place sandwiches on grill. Close lid, but do not latch. Cook until golden brown, about 1 to 2 minutes. Brush grill again with oil. Turn sandwiches and cook until golden brown, about 1 to 2 minutes. Makes 2 sandwiches.

*Suggested seasonings for chicken are: anise, basil, bay leaf, dill, fennel, garlic, lemon balm, marjoram, oregano, parsley, poultry seasoning, rosemary, sage, tarragon and thyme.*

# Hot Turkey Royale

*A superb way to use leftover turkey.*

1 (8-1/4-oz.) can asparagus spears
2 tablespoons butter or margarine
2 slices cooked turkey
2 slices whole-wheat bread
1 tablespoon all-purpose flour

1/2 cup chicken broth
1 tablespoon dry white wine
Salt and pepper to taste
2 tablespoons crumbled blue cheese

Prepare unit for open grilling. On preheated grill, cook and turn asparagus in liquid until heated through, about 3 minutes. Remove, drain and keep warm. Melt butter or margarine on grill. Cook and turn turkey in butter or margarine until heated through, about 2 minutes. Spoon asparagus on top of turkey; roll up. Place on bread slices. Stir flour into juices on grill. In a small bowl, mix chicken broth and wine; stir into flour mixture on grill. Cook and stir until mixture thickens, about 2 minutes. Season to taste with salt and pepper. Spoon sauce over turkey and asparagus on bread. Sprinkle with blue cheese. Makes 2 open-face sandwiches.

# Hot Tuna Sandwiches

*Grapes and pineapple slices move tuna up on the gourmet scale.*

1 tablespoon vegetable oil
1/2 cup seedless green grapes
2 tablespoons chopped onion
2 tablespoons chopped celery
1/4 cup Thousand Island dressing
1 (6-1/2-oz.) can tuna, drained

1 hard-boiled egg, chopped
Crisp lettuce leaves
6 slices white bread
3 slices pineapple
Celery salt

Prepare unit for open grilling. Add oil to preheated grill. Cook grapes, onion and celery in oil until onions are clear, about 3 minutes. Place in a bowl; keep warm. Add dressing to grill. Cook and stir tuna and egg in dressing until heated through, about 3 minutes. Add to grape mixture; mix well. Place lettuce leaves on 3 bread slices. Top with tuna mixture and pineapple slices. Sprinkle with celery salt. Cover with remaining bread slices. Makes 3 sandwiches.

# Shrimp Cocktail in a Bun

*For an appetizer, serve the shrimp on wooden picks with a bowl of Cocktail Sauce.*

1/4 cup vegetable oil
1 (9-oz.) pkg. frozen breaded shrimp sticks
3 hamburger rolls

Boston lettuce leaves
Cocktail Sauce, see below

*Cocktail Sauce:*
1/4 cup chili sauce
1 tablespoon prepared horseradish
1 tablespoon chopped onion

1 teaspoon lemon juice
1/2 teaspoon Worcestershire sauce

Prepare unit for open grilling. Add oil to preheated grill. Cook shrimp sticks in hot oil until brown or shrimp flakes easily with a fork, 2 to 2-1/2 minutes, turning several times. Serve on hamburger rolls with lettuce leaves and Cocktail Sauce. Makes 3 sandwiches.

Cocktail Sauce:

Prepare unit for open grilling. Combine chili sauce, horseradish, onion, lemon juice and Worcestershire sauce. Cook and stir on preheated grill until heated through, about 1-1/2 minutes. Makes 1/3 cup sauce.

## How to Make Shrimp Cocktail in a Bun

1/Cook shrimp sticks in hot oil on the grill, turning often so they brown evenly. When done they will flake easily with a fork.

2/Line bottoms of hamburger rolls with lettuce. Place crisp shrimp sticks on lettuce. Top with hot Cocktail Sauce.

# Bagels With Creamy Salmon Filling

*Blend lox and cheese to make a creamy filling for your bagels.*

2 tablespoons butter or margarine
2 bagels, split
2 oz. smoked salmon, flaked

1 (3-oz.) pkg. cream cheese, softened
2 tablespoons chopped pimiento

Prepare unit for open grilling. Melt butter or margarine on preheated grill. Add bagel tops and cook until toasted, about 1/2 minute. Remove and repeat with bagel bottoms. Cook and stir salmon in butter or margarine on grill until heated through, about 1-1/2 minutes. Add more butter or margarine if needed. Remove and mix with cream cheese and pimiento in a small bowl. Spread salmon mixture on bagel bottoms. Top with bagel tops. Makes 2 sandwiches.

# Vegetarian Delight

*A delicious nutrition-packed sandwich with freshness and crunch.*

3 tablespoons butter or margarine
2 sesame seed hamburger rolls, split
2 slices Muenster cheese
2 slices sharp Cheddar cheese
1/4 cup chopped onion
1/2 medium carrot, grated

1/4 cup Italian salad dressing
Celery salt
6 slices cucumber
4 slices tomato
1/4 cup alfalfa sprouts

Prepare unit for open grilling. On preheated grill, melt butter or margarine. Place top of hamburger rolls on grill, split side down. Cook until toasted, about 1/2 minute. Remove and top with Muenster cheese slices. Cook bottoms of hamburger rolls, split side down, until toasted, about 1/2 minute. Remove and top with Cheddar cheese slices. Cook and stir onion, carrot, salad dressing and celery salt on grill until vegetables are crisp-tender, about 2 minutes. Layer bottoms of hamburger rolls with cucumber slices and tomato slices. Spoon onion-carrot mixture on top of tomatoes. Top with alfalfa sprouts. Cover with hamburger roll tops. Makes 2 sandwiches.

# Grilled Guacamole Sandwiches

*Enjoy the rich nutlike flavor of avocados!*

1 avocado, peeled, seeded and mashed
2 tablespoons chopped onion
2 tablespoons canned chopped chilies
2 tablespoons mayonnaise
1 teaspoon lemon juice

4 slices cracked-wheat bread
1 tablespoon butter or margarine, softened
4 thin slices tomato
2 slices Monterey Jack cheese
1 tablespoon butter or margarine

Prepare unit for open grilling. In a medium bowl, mix avocado, onion, chilies, mayonnaise and lemon juice. Spread on 2 bread slices. Spread remaining bread slices with 1 tablespoon butter or margarine. Top avocado filling with tomato and cheese. Cover with remaining bread slices, buttered side up. Melt 1 tablespoon butter or margarine on preheated grill. Cook sandwiches, buttered side up, in butter or margarine until golden brown, 1-1/2 to 2 minutes on each side. Makes 2 sandwiches.

# Grilled Apple Butter Sandwiches

*Something different for the peanut butter crowd.*

2 slices bacon, chopped
1/4 cup apple butter
2 tablespoons peanut butter

4 slices raisin or cinnamon bread
2 tablespoons butter or margarine, softened

Prepare unit for open grilling. Cook bacon on preheated grill until crisp, about 2 minutes. Drain grill. In a small bowl, mix bacon, apple butter and peanut butter. Spread mixture on 2 bread slices. Cover with remaining bread slices. Spread butter or margarine on both sides of sandwiches. Cook on grill until golden brown, about 1 minute on each side. Makes 2 sandwiches.

---

*Suggested seasonings for lamb are: bay leaf, basil, chervil, coriander, dill, fennel, garlic, lemon balm, mint, oregano, parsley, rosemary, sage, savory, tansy, tarragon and thyme.*

# *Barbecue Pork Sandwiches*

*Turn leftover pork roast into a delicious hot sandwich.*

1/2 cup ketchup
2 tablespoons water
1 tablespoon Worcestershire sauce
2 teaspoons brown sugar

Dash garlic powder
Dash bottled hot pepper sauce
2 large slices cooked pork roast
2 hamburger rolls

Prepare unit for open grilling. In a small bowl, mix ketchup, water, Worcestershire sauce, brown sugar, garlic powder and hot pepper sauce. Pour onto preheated grill; add pork. Cook until pork is heated through, about 2 minutes, turning pork and spooning sauce over several times. Serve on hamburger rolls. Makes 2 sandwiches.

# *Grilled Cheese & Bacon Sandwiches*

*A hearty sandwich that's long on flavor.*

1/2 cup shredded process American cheese,
  (2-oz.)
2 tablespoons mayonnaise
2 tablespoons chopped pimiento

2 tablespoons bacon bits
4 white bread slices
Butter or margarine, softened

Prepare unit for closed grilling. In a small bowl, mix cheese, mayonnaise, pimiento and bacon bits. Spread 1 side of each bread slice with butter or margarine. Spread unbuttered side of 2 bread slices with cheese mixture. Top with remaining bread slices, buttered side out. Place sandwiches on preheated grill. Close lid, but do not latch. Cook until golden brown, about 1 minute on each side. Makes 2 sandwiches.

# *Pancakes*

Pancakes cook beautifully on your mini-grill! They seem made for each other. So keep a batch of pancake batter in the refrigerator. Sleepyheads and morning stragglers can cook their own pancakes when they get around to it. And you'll always have the option of pancakes for lunch, supper or a snack.

Try the recipe for Basic Pancakes and add whatever fresh fruits are in season. Fruit-flavored yogurts are also good—nutritious, too. Whatever you do, don't cool off your pancakes by using cold syrup right from the refrigerator. Heat it up first—just pour it right on your mini-grill. The chill will be gone in less than a minute. If peanut butter and jelly is your thing, don't let the week go by without sampling Peanut Butter & Jelly Stack-Ups.

Pancakes are a huge success as a dessert. The next time you entertain, serve Rocky Road Pancakes. Or how about Peach Melba Pancakes or Strawberry Yogurt Stack-Ups?

Want to give a brunch? Let Orange-Ambrosia Foldovers or Zucchini Pancakes be the main attraction. Why not have several different pancake batters for your guests to choose from? Then let them cook their own!

# Basic Pancakes

*Plain and simple—the all-time favorite!*

1 cup all-purpose flour
1 tablespoon baking powder
1 tablespoon sugar
1/2 teaspoon salt

1 egg, beaten
1 cup milk
2 tablespoons vegetable oil
Vegetable oil

Prepare unit for open grilling. In a medium bowl, mix flour, baking powder, sugar and salt. In a small bowl, combine egg, milk and 2 tablespoons oil. Add to flour mixture. Stir until moistened. Brush preheated grill with oil. Using 1/4 cup batter for each pancake, cook on grill until underside is golden brown and surface is bubbly, about 1-1/2 minutes. Turn and cook until other side is golden brown, about another 1-1/2 minutes. Makes 8 pancakes.

**Variation**
**Silver Dollar Pancakes:** Use 1 tablespoon rather than 1/4 cup batter for each silver dollar pancake. Cook on preheated grill until underside is golden brown and surface is bubbly, about 1 minute. Turn and cook until other side is golden brown, about another minute. Makes 28 silver dollar pancakes.

# Buttermilk Pancakes

*Fluffy and light—mother never made them this good!*

1 cup all-purpose flour
1 tablespoon sugar
2 teaspoons baking powder
1/2 teaspoon baking soda
1/2 teaspoon salt

1 egg, beaten
1 cup buttermilk
2 tablespoons vegetable oil
Vegetable oil

Prepare unit for open grilling. In a medium bowl, mix flour, sugar, baking powder, baking soda and salt. In a small bowl, combine egg, buttermilk and 2 tablespoons oil. Add to flour mixture. Stir until moistened. Brush preheated grill with oil. Using 1/4 cup of batter for each pancake, cook on grill until underside is golden brown and surface is bubbly, about 1-1/2 minutes. Turn and cook until other side is golden brown, about another 1-1/2 minutes. Makes 8 pancakes.

# Whole-Wheat Pancakes

*Chock-full of fiber. Don't miss the Oatmeal-Raisin variation!*

| | |
|---|---|
| 1/2 cup all-purpose flour | 1 egg, beaten |
| 1/2 cup whole-wheat flour | 1 cup milk |
| 1 tablespoon baking powder | 2 tablespoons vegetable oil |
| 1 tablespoon sugar | Vegetable oil |
| 1/2 teaspoon salt | |

Prepare unit for open grilling. In a medium bowl, mix flours, baking powder, sugar and salt. In a small bowl, combine egg, milk and 2 tablespoons oil. Add to flour mixture. Stir until moistened. Brush preheated grill with oil. Using 1/4 cup batter for each pancake, cook on grill until underside is golden brown and surface is bubbly, about 1-1/2 minutes. Turn and cook until other side is golden brown, about another 1-1/2 minutes. Makes 8 pancakes.

**Variation**
**Oatmeal-Raisin Pancakes:** Substitute 1/2 cup quick-cooking oats for the whole-wheat flour, reduce milk to 3/4 cup and stir in 1/2 cup raisins.

## How to Make Whole-Wheat Pancakes

1/Mix pancake ingredients until just moistened. Do not overstir—some lumps should remain in the batter.

2/Pancakes are ready to turn when small bubbles appear all over the surface. The bottom side should be nicely browned.

# *Buttermilk Corncakes*

*Buttermilk and cornmeal—wholesome country flavors.*

2/3 cup yellow corn meal
1/3 cup all-purpose flour
1 teaspoon baking soda
1 teaspoon sugar
1/2 teaspoon salt

1 egg, beaten
1 cup buttermilk
2 tablespoons vegetable oil
Vegetable oil

Prepare unit for open grilling. In a medium bowl, mix corn meal, flour, baking soda, sugar and salt. In a small bowl, mix egg, buttermilk and 2 tablespoons oil. Add to flour mixture. Stir until moistened. Brush preheated grill with oil. Using 1/4 cup batter for each pancake, cook on grill until underside is golden brown and surface is bubbly, about 1-1/2 minutes. Turn and cook until other side is golden brown, about another 1-1/2 minutes. Makes 8 pancakes.

# *Ricotta Pancakes*

*Eggs and ricotta cheese make a light but satisfying pancake.*

3 eggs, separated
8 oz. ricotta cheese
2/3 cup milk
1/2 cup all-purpose flour

1 teaspoon baking powder
Vegetable oil
Powdered sugar and jam *or* maple syrup

Prepare unit for open grilling. Beat egg whites with electric mixer on high speed until stiff, but not dry; tips should stand straight. In a medium bowl, beat egg yolks until very thick and lemon-colored. Add cheese, milk, flour and baking powder. Stir until large lumps disappear. Fold in beaten egg whites. Brush preheated grill with oil. Using 1/4 cup batter for each pancake, cook on grill until underside is golden brown and surface is bubbly, about 1 minute. Turn and cook until other side is golden brown, about another minute. Top with powdered sugar and jam or maple syrup. Makes 15 pancakes.

*If you need buttermilk for a recipe, but don't have any on hand, make your own. To make 1 cup buttermilk, combine 1 tablespoon vinegar with enough sweet milk to make 1 cup. Let stand a few minutes before using.*

# Granola Crunch Pancakes

*Use a rolling pin to crush granola between sheets of wax paper.*

Vegetable oil                                  1 cup crushed granola
2 cups Basic Pancake batter, page 63, or
   Buttermilk Pancake batter, page 63

Prepare unit for open grilling. Brush preheated grill with oil. Using 1/4 cup batter for each pancake, pour onto grill. Sprinkle each pancake with 2 tablespoons granola. Cook until underside is golden brown and surface is bubbly, about 1-1/2 minutes. Turn and cook until other side is golden brown, about another 1-1/2 minutes. Makes 8 pancakes.

### Variations

**Blueberry Pancakes:** Substitute 1 cup fresh, thawed frozen, or drained canned blueberries and 1 tablespoon sugar for the granola.
**Pineapple Pancakes:** Substitute 1 (8-oz.) can drained, crushed pineapple for the granola.
**Apple-Cinnamon Pancakes:** Substitute 1 cup thinly sliced, pared, cored apple with 1 tablespoon sugar and 1 teaspoon ground cinnamon for the granola.
**Spiced Peach Pancakes:** Substitute 1 cup chopped canned spiced peaches for the granola.
**Cranberry Pancakes:** Substitute 1 cup chopped cranberries and 2 tablespoons sugar for the granola.

## How to Make Granola Crunch Pancakes

**1/Use a 1/4 cup measure to pour pancake batter onto the grill. This will help make the pancakes a uniform size.**

**2/Sprinkle on granola, blueberries or other fruit as soon as you spoon batter onto the grill.**

# Honey-Nut Hotcakes

*This is a special occasion pancake!*

1 cup all-purpose flour
1 tablespoon baking powder
1/2 teaspoon salt
1 egg, beaten
1 cup milk

2 tablespoons vegetable oil
2 tablespoons honey
Vegetable oil
1 cup chopped walnuts
Honey or maple syrup

Prepare unit for open grilling. In a medium bowl, mix flour, baking powder and salt. In a small bowl, combine egg, milk, 2 tablespoons oil and 2 tablespoons honey. Add to flour mixture. Stir until moistened. Brush preheated grill with oil. Using 1/4 cup batter for each hotcake, pour onto grill. Sprinkle each hotcake with 2 tablespoons walnuts. Cook until underside is golden brown and surface is bubbly, about 1-1/2 minutes. Turn and cook until other side is golden brown, about 1-1/2 minutes. Top with honey or maple syrup. Makes 8 hotcakes.

# Applesauce Pancakes

*Stir a little cinnamon-sugar into some applesauce and spoon on top of pancakes.*

1 cup all-purpose flour
1 tablespoon baking powder
1 tablespoon sugar
1 teaspoon ground cinnamon
1/2 teaspoon salt

1 egg, beaten
3/4 cup milk
1/3 cup applesauce
2 tablespoons vegetable oil
Vegetable oil

Prepare unit for open grilling. In a medium bowl, mix flour, baking powder, sugar, cinnamon and salt. In a small bowl, combine egg, milk, applesauce and 2 tablespoons oil. Add to flour mixture. Stir until moistened. Brush preheated grill with oil. Using 1/4 cup batter for each pancake, cook on grill until underside is golden brown and surface is bubbly, about 1-1/2 minutes. Turn and cook until other side is golden brown, about another 1-1/2 minutes. Makes 8 pancakes.

---

*Pancakes topped with warmed syrup brighten up any morning. You can heat 1 cup of syrup on the preheated open grill in 1-1/2 to 2 minutes. Stir syrup occasionally while heating.*

# Blueberry-Lemon Deluxe Pancakes

*Lemon yogurt gives blueberry pancakes magnificent texture and delectable flavor.*

1 cup all-purpose flour
2 tablespoons sugar
1 tablespoon baking powder
1/2 teaspoon salt
1/4 teaspoon baking soda
1 egg, beaten
1/2 cup milk
1/2 cup lemon yogurt

2 tablespoons vegetable oil
Vegetable oil
1 cup fresh, thawed frozen, or
    drained canned blueberries
1/2 cup lemon yogurt
1/4 cup fresh, thawed frozen, or
    drained canned blueberries

Prepare unit for open grilling. In a medium bowl, mix flour, sugar, baking powder, salt and baking soda. In a small bowl, combine egg, milk, 1/2 cup lemon yogurt and 2 tablespoons oil. Add to flour mixture. Stir until moistened. Brush preheated grill with oil. Using 1/4 cup batter for each pancake, pour onto grill. Sprinkle each pancake with 2 tablespoons blueberries. Cook until underside is golden brown and surface is bubbly, about 2 minutes. Turn and cook until other side is golden brown, about 2 minutes. Top with remaining yogurt and garnish with remaining blueberries. Makes 8 pancakes.

# Peach Melba Pancakes

*Invite a friend over for brunch.*

1 (8-oz.) can peach slices
1 cup all-purpose flour
2 tablespoons baking powder
1 tablespoon sugar
1/2 teaspoon salt
1 egg, beaten

3/4 cup milk
2 tablespoons vegetable oil
Vegetable oil
1 (10-oz.) pkg. frozen sweetened raspberries,
    thawed
1 cup whipped topping

Prepare unit for open grilling. Drain peaches; reserve 2 tablespoons liquid. Chop peaches into small pieces. In a medium bowl, mix flour, baking powder, sugar and salt. In a small bowl, combine egg, milk, 2 tablespoons oil and reserved liquid. Add to flour mixture. Add chopped peaches; stir until moistened. Brush preheated grill with oil. Using 1/4 cup batter for each pancake, cook on grill until underside is golden brown and surface is bubbly, about 1-1/2 minutes. Turn and cook until other side is golden brown, about another 1-1/2 minutes. Top with raspberries and a dollop of whipped topping. Makes 8 pancakes.

# *Hawaiian Hotcakes*

*You can almost hear the surf breaking on the shore.*

1 cup all-purpose flour
2 tablespoons baking powder
2 tablespoons sugar
1/2 teaspoon salt
1 egg, beaten
1 cup milk

2 tablespoons vegetable oil
1 (8-oz.) can crushed pineapple, drained
1/2 cup shredded coconut
Vegetable oil
Pineapple Sauce, see below
Shredded coconut, for garnish

*Pineapple Sauce:*
1/2 cup sugar
1 tablespoon cornstarch

1 cup pineapple juice
2 tablespoons lemon juice

Prepare unit for open grilling. In a medium bowl, mix flour, baking powder, 2 tablespoons sugar and salt. In a small bowl, combine egg, milk and 2 tablespoons oil. Add to flour mixture. Stir until moistened. In another small bowl, mix pineapple and 1/2 cup coconut. Brush preheated grill with oil. Using 1/4 cup batter for each hotcake, pour onto grill. Sprinkle each hotcake with 2 table-spoons pineapple-coconut mixture. Cook until underside is golden brown and surface is bubbly, about 1-1/2 minutes. Turn and cook until other side is golden brown, about 1-1/2 minutes. Keep warm. Make Pineapple Sauce. Top hotcakes with Pineapple Sauce and shredded coconut. Makes 8 hotcakes.

**Pineapple Sauce:**
Prepare unit for open grilling. In a small bowl, mix 1/2 cup sugar and cornstarch. Add to cold grill. Stir in pineapple juice. Plug in grill. Cook and stir until thickened and clear, 2 to 3 minutes. Stir in lemon juice. Makes 1 cup.

# *Chocolate-Pecan Pancakes*

*These pancakes should satisfy your sweet tooth. Top with Creamy Topping, page 74.*

2 cups Basic Pancake batter, page 63
1 teaspoon vanilla extract
1/2 (6-oz.) pkg. chocolate chips (1/2 cup)

1/4 cup chopped pecans
Vegetable oil

Prepare unit for open grilling. Prepare Basic Pancake batter. Add vanilla extract, chocolate chips and pecans. Stir until moistened. Brush preheated grill with oil. Using 1/4 cup batter for each pancake, cook on grill until underside is golden brown and surface is bubbly, about 1-1/2 minutes. Turn and cook until other side is golden brown, about another 1-1/2 minutes. Makes 10 pancakes.

**Variation**
**Cashew Scotchies:** Substitute 1/2 cup butterscotch chips and 1/4 cup chopped cashews for the chocolate chips and pecans.

# Strawberry-Yogurt Stack-Ups

*These fabulous stacks are filled with creamy yogurt and juicy strawberries.*

1 (10-oz.) pkg. frozen sweetened strawberries, thawed
1 cup all-purpose flour
1 tablespoon baking powder
1/2 teaspoon salt

1 egg, beaten
3/4 cup milk
1 tablespoon vegetable oil
Vegetable oil
1 (8-oz.) carton plain yogurt

Prepare unit for open grilling. Drain strawberries; reserve 2 tablespoons syrup. In a medium bowl, mix flour, baking powder and salt. In a small bowl, combine egg, milk, 1 tablespoon oil and reserved syrup. Add to flour mixture. Add 1/4 cup of the strawberries; stir until moistened. Brush pre-heated grill with oil. Using 1/4 cup batter for each pancake, cook on grill until underside is golden brown and surface is bubbly, about 1-1/2 minutes. Turn and cook until other side is golden brown, about another 1-1/2 minutes. Using 4 pancakes for each stack, layer yogurt and remaining straw-berries between pancakes; reserve 2 strawberries for garnish. Top with a dollop of yogurt and re-served strawberries. Makes 2 stack-ups.

# Sour Cream & Raisin Cakes

*Exquisite cream-filled pancake sandwiches are good enough for dessert!*

Fluffy Raisin Filling, see below
1 cup all-purpose flour
2 tablespoons sugar
1 tablespoon baking powder
1/2 teaspoon salt
1/2 teaspoon ground nutmeg

1/4 teaspoon baking soda
1 egg, beaten
1/2 cup milk
1/2 cup dairy sour cream
1 tablespoon vegetable oil
Vegetable oil

*Fluffy Raisin Filling:*
1 cup whipped topping
1/4 cup dairy sour cream

2 tablespoons raisins
1/2 teaspoon ground nutmeg

Prepare Fluffy Raisin Filling; set aside. Prepare unit for open grilling. In a medium bowl, mix flour, sugar, baking powder, salt, 1/2 teaspoon nutmeg and baking soda. In a small bowl, combine egg, milk, 1/2 cup sour cream and 1 tablespoon oil. Add to flour mixture. Stir until moistened. Brush preheated grill with oil. Using 1/4 cup batter for each pancake, cook on grill until underside is golden brown and surface is bubbly, about 1-1/2 minutes. Turn and cook until other side is golden brown, about 1-1/2 minutes. Spread 4 pancakes with Fluffy Raisin Filling and cover with remaining pan-cakes. Makes 4 pancake sandwiches.

**Fluffy Raisin Filling:**
In a medium bowl, mix whipped topping, 1/4 cup sour cream, raisins and 1/2 teaspoon nutmeg. Stir to blend well. Makes about 1-1/4 cups.

# Rocky Road Pancakes

*A chocolate-lover's dream come true.*

1/2 cup all-purpose flour
2 tablespoons cocoa powder
1 tablespoon sugar
1-1/2 teaspoons baking powder
1/4 teaspoon salt
1 egg, beaten
1/3 cup milk

1 tablespoon vegetable oil
1/4 cup miniature marshmallows
1/4 cup pecan halves
Vegetable oil
Vanilla ice cream
Chocolate syrup
Pecans for garnish, if desired

Prepare unit for open grilling. In a medium bowl, mix flour, cocoa, sugar, baking powder and salt. In a small bowl, combine egg, milk and 1 tablespoon oil. Add to flour mixture. Add marshmallows and 1/4 cup pecans. Stir until moistened. Brush preheated grill with oil. Using 1/4 cup batter for each pancake, cook on preheated grill until underside is golden brown and surface is bubbly, about 1-1/2 minutes. Turn and cook until other side is golden brown, about 1-1/2 minutes. Top with ice cream and chocolate syrup. Sprinkle with pecans, if desired. Makes 4 pancakes.

# Orange-Ambrosia Foldovers

*Set aside a few spoonfuls of Ambrosia Filling to top the foldovers.*

Ambrosia Filling, see below
1 cup all-purpose flour
1 tablespoon baking powder
1 tablespoon sugar
1 teaspoon grated orange peel

1/2 teaspoon salt
1 egg, beaten
1 cup milk
2 tablespoons vegetable oil
Vegetable oil

*Ambrosia Filling:*
1 (11-oz.) can mandarin orange sections, drained
1 (8-oz.) can crushed pineapple, drained

1/2 cup flaked coconut
1 cup whipped topping

Prepare Ambrosia Filling; set aside. Prepare unit for open grilling. In a medium bowl, mix flour, baking powder, sugar, orange peel and salt. In a small bowl, combine egg, milk and 2 tablespoons oil. Add to flour mixture. Stir until moistened. Brush preheated grill with oil. Using 1/4 cup batter for each pancake, cook on grill until underside is golden brown and surface is bubbly, about 1-1/2 minutes. Turn and cook until other side is golden brown, about 1-1/2 minutes. Place about 2 tablespoons Ambrosia Filling onto 1 side of each pancake. Fold over and secure with wooden picks. Makes 8 filled pancakes.

Ambrosia Filling:
In a medium bowl, fold orange sections, pineapple and coconut into whipped topping. Makes about 2 cups filling.

# Pumpkin Delights

*Good for breakfast or dessert!*

1 cup all-purpose flour
3 tablespoons sugar
1 tablespoon baking powder
1/2 teaspoon salt
1/2 teaspoon ground cinnamon
1/2 teaspoon ground cloves
1/2 teaspoon ground nutmeg

1 egg, beaten
1 cup milk
1/2 cup canned pumpkin
2 tablespoons vegetable oil
Vegetable oil
1 cup whipped topping

Prepare unit for open grilling. In a medium bowl, mix flour, sugar, baking powder, salt, cinnamon, cloves and nutmeg. In a small bowl, combine egg, milk, pumpkin and 2 tablespoons oil. Add to flour mixture. Stir until moistened. Brush preheated grill with oil. Using 1/4 cup batter for each pancake, cook on grill until underside is golden brown and surface is bubbly, about 1-1/2 minutes. Turn and cook until other side is golden brown, about 1-1/2 minutes. Top with whipped topping. Makes 10 pancakes.

# Creamy Banana-Nut Cakes

*If you're like me, you won't be able to wait for a special occasion to try these.*

Creamy Topping, see below
1 cup all-purpose flour
1 tablespoon baking powder
1 tablespoon sugar
1/2 teaspoon salt
1 egg, beaten

1 cup milk
1 medium banana, mashed
1 tablespoon vegetable oil
1/2 cup chopped pecans
Vegetable oil

*Creamy Topping:*
1 (3-oz.) pkg. cream cheese, softened
1/2 cup whipped topping

Prepare Creamy Topping; set aside. Prepare unit for open grilling. In a medium bowl, mix flour, baking powder, sugar and salt. In a small bowl, combine egg, milk, banana and 1 tablespoon oil. Add to flour mixture. Sprinkle with pecans; stir until moistened. Brush preheated grill with oil. Using 1/4 cup batter for each pancake, cook on grill until underside is golden brown and surface is bubbly, about 1-1/2 minutes. Turn and cook until other side is golden brown, about another 1-1/2 minutes. Top with Creamy Topping. Makes 10 pancakes.

**Creamy Topping:**
In a small bowl, beat cream cheese with electric mixer on high speed until light and fluffy. Fold in whipped topping. Makes 1 cup topping.

# Sweet Potato Cakes

*Delicious with butter and maple syrup.*

1 cup all-purpose flour
1 tablespoon baking powder
1 tablespoon sugar
1 teaspoon ground allspice
1/2 teaspoon salt

1 egg, beaten
1 cup milk
1/3 cup cooked mashed sweet potato
2 tablespoons vegetable oil
Vegetable oil

Prepare unit for open grilling. In a medium bowl, mix flour, baking powder, sugar, allspice and salt. In a small bowl, combine egg, milk, sweet potato and 2 tablespoons oil. Add to flour mixture. Stir until moistened. Brush preheated grill with oil. Using 1/4 cup batter for each pancake, cook on grill until underside is golden brown and surface is bubbly, about 1-1/2 minutes. Turn and cook until other side is golden brown, about 1-1/2 minutes. Makes 9 pancakes.

# Zucchini Pancakes

*What a clever way to use zucchini! Serve with sausage for a superb lunch.*

1 egg, beaten
2 cups finely grated zucchini (2 medium)
2 tablespoons grated Parmesan cheese
1 tablespoon all-purpose flour
1 teaspoon snipped fresh parsley

1/4 teaspoon garlic salt
1/4 teaspoon salt
1/8 teaspoon pepper
Vegetable oil
Maple syrup

Prepare unit for open grilling. In a medium bowl, mix egg, zucchini, Parmesan cheese, flour, parsley, garlic salt, salt and pepper. Mix well. Brush preheated grill with oil. Using 1/4 cup batter for each pancake, cook on grill until underside is golden brown and surface is bubbly, about 1-1/2 to 2 minutes. Turn and cook until other side is golden brown, about 1-1/2 to 2 minutes. Stir mixture before spooning remaining batter onto grill. Top with maple syrup. Makes 6 pancakes.

---

*Honey butter makes an extra-special pancake topping. Beat 1/2 cup butter with electric mixer on high speed until fluffy. Gradually add 1/4 cup honey and beat until smooth.*

---

# Peanut Butter & Jelly Stack-Ups

*An unbeatable combination for kids from 1 to 100!*

1 cup all-purpose flour
1 tablespoon baking powder
1 tablespoon sugar
1/2 teaspoon salt
1 egg, beaten
1 cup milk

1/3 cup chunk-style peanut butter
2 tablespoons vegetable oil
Vegetable oil
1-1/2 cups grape jelly
About 2 tablespoons peanut butter
1/4 cup chopped peanuts

Prepare unit for open grilling. In a medium bowl, mix flour, baking powder, sugar and salt. In a small bowl, combine egg, milk, 1/3 cup peanut butter and 2 tablespoons oil. Add to flour mixture. Stir until moistened. Brush preheated grill with oil. Using 1/4 cup batter for each pancake, cook on grill until underside is golden brown and surface is bubbly, about 1-1/2 minutes. Turn and cook until other side is golden brown, about 1-1/2 minutes. Use 4 pancakes for each stack. Spread jelly on 3 pancakes and cover with fourth pancake. Spread top with peanut butter. Add a dollop of jelly and sprinkle with peanuts. Makes 2 stack-ups.

## How to Make Peanut Butter & Jelly Stack-Ups

**1/Let the kids spread peanut butter pancakes with their favorite jelly.**

**2/Stack them as high as you like—then top with more peanut butter, jelly and peanuts.**

# *Spanish Pancakes*

*For a zesty south-of-the-border treat, serve with taco sauce and chorizo—spicy Mexican sausage.*

1 cup all-purpose flour
1 tablespoon baking powder
1 tablespoon sugar
1/2 teaspoon salt
1 egg, beaten
1 cup milk

2 tablespoons vegetable oil
1/4 cup drained canned or thawed frozen
  corn
2 tablespoons chopped green or red pepper
1 teaspoon dehydrated minced onion flakes
Vegetable oil

Prepare unit for open grilling. In a medium bowl, mix flour, baking powder, sugar and salt. In a small bowl, combine egg, milk and 2 tablespoons oil. Add to flour mixture. Add corn, pepper and onion flakes. Stir until moistened. Brush preheated grill with oil. Using 1/4 cup batter for each pancake, cook on grill until underside is golden brown and surface is bubbly, about 1-1/2 minutes. Turn and cook until other side is golden brown, about 1-1/2 minutes. Makes 10 pancakes.

# *Sausage & Cheese Pancakes*

*For hearty appetites!*

4 oz. bulk pork sausage
1 cup all-purpose flour
1 tablespoon baking powder
1 tablespoon sugar
1/2 teaspoon salt

1 egg, beaten
1 cup milk
2 tablespoons vegetable oil
1/4 cup shredded process American cheese
  (1-oz.)

Prepare unit for open grilling. Crumble sausage onto preheated grill. Cook and stir until sausage is brown, about 3 minutes. Remove sausage and set aside. Drain drippings from grill. In a medium bowl, mix flour, baking powder, sugar and salt. In a small bowl, combine egg, milk and oil. Add to flour mixture. Add sausage and cheese; stir until moistened. Using 1/4 cup batter for each pancake, cook on grill until underside is brown and surface is bubbly, about 1-1/2 minutes. Turn and cook until other side is brown, about 1-1/2 minutes. Makes 10 pancakes.

# Chicken Stack-Ups

*This will taste good morning, noon or night.*

| | |
|---|---|
| 2 tablespoons butter or margarine | 2 teaspoons baking powder |
| 1/4 cup chopped fresh mushrooms | 2 teaspoons sugar |
| 3 tablespoons chopped onion | 1/4 teaspoon salt |
| 3 tablespoons chopped green pepper | 1 egg, beaten |
| 1/2 cup cubed cooked chicken | 1/2 cup milk |
| 1/2 cup condensed cream of chicken soup | 1 tablespoon vegetable oil |
| 2 tablespoons water | Vegetable oil |
| 1/2 cup all-purpose flour | 2 green pepper rings |

Prepare unit for open grilling. Melt butter or margarine on preheated grill. Add mushrooms, onion and 3 tablespoons green pepper. Cook and stir until tender, about 5 minutes. Add chicken, soup and water. Cook and stir until heated through, about 2 minutes. Remove and keep warm. In a medium bowl, mix flour, baking powder, sugar and salt. In a small bowl, combine egg, milk and 1 tablespoon oil. Add to flour mixture. Stir until moistened. Brush grill with oil. Using 1/4 cup batter for each pancake, cook on grill until underside is golden brown and surface is bubbly, about 1-1/2 minutes. Turn and cook until other side is golden brown, about 1-1/2 minutes. Spread 2 pancakes with chicken filling. Cover with remaining pancakes. Garnish with green pepper rings. Makes 2 stack-ups.

# Salami Stack-Ups

*Salami and cheese between rich sour cream and cottage cheese pancakes.*

| | |
|---|---|
| 1/3 cup all-purpose flour | 1/2 cup cottage cheese |
| 1/2 teaspoon sugar | Vegetable oil |
| 1/4 teaspoon salt | Horseradish sauce |
| 1/8 teaspoon baking soda | 2 slices salami |
| 2 eggs, beaten | 2 slices process American cheese |
| 1/2 cup sour cream with chives dip | Sour cream with chives dip |

Prepare unit for open grilling. In a medium bowl, mix flour, sugar, salt and baking soda. In a small bowl, beat eggs, 1/2 cup sour cream dip and cottage cheese. Add to flour mixture. Stir until moistened. Brush preheated grill with oil. Using 1/4 cup batter for each pancake, cook on grill until underside is golden brown and surface is bubbly, about 2-1/2 minutes. Turn and cook until other side is golden brown, about 2-1/2 minutes. Spread 4 pancakes with horseradish sauce. Top with a salami slice. Cover with another pancake spread with horseradish sauce. Add a cheese slice and cover with remaining pancake. Top each stack with a dollop of sour cream dip. Makes 2 stack-ups.

# *Eggs*

Your mini-grill will make the best, easiest and most fool-proof omelets you have ever put on the table! And the fillings are limitless. Try any kind of cheese filling dashed with herbs. Add whatever you have on hand: some chopped tomato, avocado chunks, mushrooms, broccoli slices, asparagus or spinach. See how it's done in Creamy Tomato Omelet or Fresh Spring Omelet. Don't forget to heat an easy sauce on the grill to spoon over your masterpiece. Try a bit of canned soup thinned with a little wine or milk. Or use one of the many packaged sauce mixes or canned sauces you'll find in your market. Treat hearty eaters with cooked bacon, ham or sausage to go inside or alongside their omelet.

If you're not in an omelet mood, you can have your eggs either sunny-side-up or over-easy. Your grill will cook them to perfection. Or scramble an egg and toss in leftover meat or vegetables. Sprinkle on a little shredded cheese and crown it with a dab of sour cream. Delicious!

If you want to impress the brunch crowd, do it with Eggs Benedict or Huevos Rancheros. They'll be amazed.

# Oriental Omelet

*Chinese vegetables add crunchy texture and an exotic flair.*

1/2 (16-oz.) can fancy mixed Chinese
  vegetables
1 tablespoon cornstarch
1 tablespoon soy sauce
1/2 teaspoon garlic powder

4 eggs
2 tablespoons water
1/4 teaspoon salt
Dash pepper
2 tablespoons vegetable oil

Prepare unit for open grilling. Add Chinese vegetables to preheated grill. In a small bowl, mix cornstarch, soy sauce and garlic powder. Stir into Chinese vegetables. Cook and stir until thickened, about 2-1/2 minutes. Remove and keep warm. In a small bowl, beat eggs, water, salt and pepper until just blended. Add 1 tablespoon of the oil to the grill. Pour half the egg mixture onto grill. Cook, lifting egg mixture gently so uncooked portion flows underneath, until eggs are set, 2 to 2-1/2 minutes. Spoon half the Chinese vegetable filling onto omelet; roll up. Add remaining oil to grill. Repeat with remaining egg mixture and Chinese vegetable filling. Makes 2 servings.

# Omelet Divan

*Easy cheese sauce with broccoli rounds out this appealing and nutritious omelet.*

1 (10-oz.) pkg. frozen broccoli in cheese
  sauce, thawed
4 eggs
2 tablespoons milk

1/2 teaspoon celery salt
Dash pepper
2 tablespoons vegetable oil

Prepare unit for open grilling. On preheated grill, cook and stir broccoli in cheese sauce until heated through, about 3 minutes. Remove and keep warm. In a small bowl, beat eggs, milk, celery salt and pepper until just blended. Add 1 tablespoon of the oil to grill. Pour half the egg mixture onto grill. Cook, lifting egg mixture gently so uncooked portion flows underneath, until eggs are set, 2 to 2-1/2 minutes. Spoon half the broccoli filling onto omelet; roll up. Add remaining oil to grill. Repeat with remaining egg mixture and broccoli filling. Makes 2 servings.

*Cooking for someone on a cholesterol-free diet? There's no need to pass up delicious egg recipes. Use the cholesterol-free egg substitutes and check the label for equivalent amounts. The substitutes work especially well for omelets and scrambled dishes.*

# Sausage & Sour Cream Omelet

*This rich omelet is one of my favorites.*

8 oz. bulk pork sausage
2 tablespoons chopped green onion
1/2 cup dairy sour cream
4 eggs

2 tablespoons water
1/2 teaspoon celery salt
1 tablespoon vegetable oil

Prepare unit for open grilling. On preheated grill, cook and stir sausage and onion until sausage is brown, about 4-1/2 minutes. Remove sausage mixture; reserve drippings on grill. In a medium bowl, combine sausage mixture and sour cream. Keep warm. Beat eggs, water and celery salt until just blended. Pour half the egg mixture onto grill. Cook, lifting egg mixture gently so uncooked portion flows underneath, until eggs are set, about 2 to 2-1/2 minutes. Spoon half the sausage filling onto omelet; roll up. Add oil to grill. Repeat with remaining egg mixture and sausage filling. Makes 2 servings.

# Fluffy Omelet With Cheese Sauce

*Serve this delicate omelet for an elegant breakfast or brunch.*

Cheese Sauce, see below
2 egg whites
1 tablespoon water

1/8 teaspoon salt
2 egg yolks
2 tablespoons vegetable oil

*Cheese Sauce:*
1/2 cup condensed Cheddar cheese soup
1/4 cup milk

1 tablespoon bacon bits
1 teaspoon parsley flakes

Prepare Cheese Sauce; set aside. Prepare unit for open grilling. In a medium bowl, beat egg whites with electric mixer on high speed, until frothy. Add water and salt. Beat until stiff, but not dry; the tips should stand straight. In a small bowl, beat yolks until very thick and lemon-colored. Fold egg yolks into whites. Add oil to preheated grill. Pour egg mixture onto grill. Cook until light golden brown, about 2-1/2 minutes. Turn carefully, using 2 spatulas, and cook until other side is light golden brown, about another 2-1/2 minutes. Top with Cheese Sauce. Makes 1 to 2 servings.

**Cheese Sauce:**
Prepare unit for open grilling. Mix soup, milk, bacon and parsley on preheated grill. Cook and stir until heated through, about 2 minutes. Remove and keep warm. Makes 2/3 cup sauce.

# *Fresh Spring Omelet*

*Tender asparagus, fresh mushrooms and dillweed add a little springtime to your breakfast.*

1 tablespoon vegetable oil
1/4 cup cooked asparagus tips
1/4 cup fresh mushroom slices
2 teaspoons snipped fresh dillweed, or
   1/2 teaspoon dried dillweed

2 eggs
1 tablespoon milk
1/4 teaspoon celery salt
Dash pepper
1/4 cup shredded sharp Cheddar cheese

Prepare unit for open grilling. Add oil to preheated grill. Add asparagus, mushrooms and dillweed. Cook and stir until heated through, about 3 minutes. Remove and keep warm. In a small bowl, beat eggs, milk, celery salt and pepper until just blended. Pour onto grill. Cook, lifting egg mixture gently so uncooked portion flows underneath, until eggs are set, 2 to 2-1/2 minutes. Spoon asparagus filling onto omelet; roll up. Sprinkle with cheese. Makes 1 serving.

# *Sausage Roll-Up*

*This protein-packed omelet will keep you going all through a busy morning.*

2 pork sausage links
2 eggs
1 tablespoon milk

1/8 teaspoon salt
Dash pepper
1 slice process American cheese

Prepare unit for open grilling. On preheated grill, cook and turn sausage until done, about 5 minutes. Remove and keep warm. In a small bowl, beat eggs, milk, salt and pepper until just blended. Pour onto grill. Cook, lifting egg mixture gently so uncooked portion flows underneath, until eggs are set, 2 to 2-1/2 minutes. Lay cheese and sausage on top of omelet; roll up. Makes 1 serving.

# Mexicali Omelet

*Avacado dip and hot pepper sauce bring Mexican sunshine to your table.*

4 eggs
2 tablespoons water
1/2 teaspoon garlic salt
1/2 teaspoon chili powder
1/8 teaspoon pepper

2 tablespoons vegetable oil
1 (6-oz.) pkg. frozen avocado dip, thawed
Dash bottled hot pepper sauce
1 tomato, peeled and chopped
1/4 cup dairy sour cream

Prepare unit for open grilling. In a medium bowl, beat eggs, water, garlic salt, chili powder and pepper until just blended. Add 1 tablespoon of the oil to preheated grill. Pour half the egg mixture onto grill. Cook, lifting eggs gently so uncooked portion flows underneath, until eggs are set, 2 to 2-1/2 minutes. In a small bowl, mix avocado dip and hot pepper sauce. Spread half the avocado mixture onto omelet. Sprinkle with half the chopped tomato and top with half the sour cream. Roll up. Repeat with remaining oil, egg mixture, avocado mixture, tomato and sour cream. Makes 2 servings.

# Creamy Tomato Omelet

*Cottage cheese and tomato make a wonderful creamy filling.*

2 tablespoons vegetable oil
1/4 cup chopped tomato
1/4 cup cottage cheese with chives
2 eggs

1 tablespoon milk
1/8 teaspoon salt
Dash pepper

Prepare unit for open grilling. Add 1 tablespoon of the oil to preheated grill. Add tomato. Cook and stir until heated through, about 1 minute. In a small bowl, mix cooked tomato and cottage cheese; set aside. In another small bowl, beat eggs, milk, salt and pepper until just blended. Add remaining oil to grill. Pour egg mixture onto grill. Cook, lifting egg mixture gently so uncooked portion flows underneath, until eggs are set, 2 to 2-1/2 minutes. Spoon cottage cheese and tomato onto omelet; roll up. Makes 1 serving.

*To make a perfect omelet, use a fork to gently lift the cooked egg portion so that the uncooked portion will flow underneath the cooked portion. Don't overstir or you'll end up with scrambled eggs!*

# Herbed Omelet

*If fresh herbs are available, use 3 times the amount of dried herbs called for in this recipe.*

| | |
|---|---|
| 1/4 cup dairy sour cream | 1/8 teaspoon salt |
| 1 teaspoon Dijon-style mustard | 1 tablespoon vegetable oil |
| 2 eggs | 1 teaspoon dried chives |
| 1 tablespoon water | 1/4 teaspoon dried chervil |

Prepare unit for open grilling. In a small bowl, mix sour cream and mustard; set aside. Beat eggs, water and salt until just blended. Add oil to preheated grill. Add herbs to oil. Pour egg mixture onto grill. Cook, lifting egg mixture gently so uncooked portion flows underneath, until eggs are set, 2 to 2-1/2 minutes. Spoon sour cream filling onto omelet; roll up. Makes 1 serving.

# Omelet Lorraine

*Quiche Lorraine—without the pie crust!*

| | |
|---|---|
| 2 slices bacon | 1 tablespoon dehydrated minced onion flakes |
| 1/4 cup shredded Gruyere or Swiss cheese | 1 tablespoon milk |
| 1 teaspoon parsley flakes | 1/8 teaspoon salt |
| 2 eggs | Dash pepper |

Prepare unit for open grilling. Cook bacon on preheated grill until crisp, about 3 minutes. Drain bacon; reserve drippings on grill. Crumble bacon and mix in a small bowl with cheese and parsley; set aside. In another small bowl, beat eggs, onion flakes, milk, salt and pepper until just blended. Cook in reserved drippings, lifting egg mixture gently so uncooked portion flows underneath, until eggs are set, 2 to 2-1/2 minutes. Spoon bacon-cheese mixture onto omelet; roll up. Makes 1 serving.

# Ham & Eggs in a Hole

*Everyone—from toddlers through teens and grandparents—enjoys this fun breakfast.*

2 slices rye bread
1 (2-1/4 oz.) can deviled ham spread
1/2 teaspoon prepared mustard

1 tablespoon vegetable oil
2 eggs
1/4 cup shredded process American cheese

Prepare unit for open grilling. Cut a small circle from the center of each bread slice with center of doughnut cutter or a small lid. In a small bowl, mix ham spread and mustard; set aside. Add oil to preheated grill. Place bread slices on grill. Break 1 egg into hole in each bread slice. Cook until eggs are set, 2 to 2-1/2 minutes. Turn gently. Spread ham mixture around egg on bread and sprinkle with cheese. Cook until ham spread is heated and egg is done, 2 to 2-1/2 minutes. Makes 2 servings.

## How to Make Ham & Eggs in a Hole

**1/Using the center of a doughnut cutter or a small lid, cut a hole in the center of rye bread slices.**

**2/Break an egg into a custard cup. Carefully pour into the hole in the bread so the yolk is in the center.**

# Spanish Omelet

*Serve with a toasted tortilla and imagine yourself in Acapulco.*

1 slice bacon, chopped
2 tablespoons chopped onion
2 tablespoons chopped green pepper
2 tablespoons fresh mushroom slices
1 clove garlic, minced
1/3 cup ketchup
2 tablespoons water

1/8 teaspoon chili powder
2 eggs
1 tablespoon water
1 tablespoon vegetable oil
Dairy sour cream
Avocado slice for garnish

Prepare unit for open grilling. On preheated grill, cook and stir bacon, onion, green pepper, mushrooms and garlic until bacon is slightly crisp, about 3 minutes. Stir in ketchup, water and chili powder. Cook and stir until heated through, about 1/2 minute. Remove and keep warm. In a small bowl, beat eggs and water until just blended. Add oil to grill. Pour egg mixture onto grill. Cook, lifting egg mixture gently so uncooked portion flows underneath, until eggs are set, 2 to 2-1/2 minutes. Spoon filling onto omelet; roll up. Top with a dollop of sour cream and garnish with avocado. Makes 1 serving.

# Frittata

*The delicious updated version of an Italian favorite.*

1 tablespoon vegetable oil
2 slices salami, cut in 2 x 1/2-inch strips
1/4 cup chopped onion
1/4 cup chopped zucchini

1 garlic clove, minced
2 eggs
Dash salt
1 tablespoon grated Parmesan cheese

Prepare unit for open grilling. Add oil to preheated grill. Add salami, onion, zucchini and garlic. Cook until tender, about 4 minutes. In a small bowl, beat eggs and salt until just combined. Pour over vegetables on grill. Cook and stir carefully until eggs are set, 2 to 3 minutes. Sprinkle with Parmesan cheese. Makes 2 servings.

# Country Scrambler

*Makes a delicious midnight supper.*

3 slices bacon
2 tablespoons chopped onion
2 tablespoons chopped green pepper
3 eggs

2 tablespoons chopped pimiento
2 tablespoons milk
2 oz. American cheese, cut in 1/4-inch cubes
   (1/2 cup)

Prepare unit for open grilling. Cook bacon on preheated grill until crisp, 3 to 4 minutes. Remove bacon; reserve 2 tablespoons drippings on grill. Crumble bacon and reserve. Cook and stir onion and green pepper in reserved drippings until just tender, about 2 minutes. In a medium bowl, beat eggs, pimiento and milk until just blended. Pour onto grill with onion and green pepper. Cook, stirring occasionally, until eggs are almost set, about 2 minutes. Stir in reserved bacon and cheese. Continue cooking and stirring until eggs are set, about 1 minute longer. Makes 2 servings.

# Eggs Benedict

*A quick version of the brunch classic.*

Mock Hollandaise Sauce, see below
1 tablespoon butter or margarine
1 English muffin, halved

2 slices Canadian bacon
1 tablespoon vegetable oil
2 eggs

*Mock Hollandaise Sauce:*
2 tablespoons butter or margarine, softened
1/2 cup mayonnaise

1 tablespoon lemon juice

Prepare Mock Hollandaise Sauce; set aside. Prepare unit for open grilling. On preheated grill, melt 1 tablespoon butter or margarine. Toast muffin halves, cut side down, until light brown, 1/2 to 1 minute. Remove and keep warm. Cook Canadian bacon until brown, 1/2 to 1 minute on each side. Place on top of muffin halves and keep warm. Add oil to grill. Break eggs onto grill. Cook until set, about 1 minute. Turn and cook to desired doneness, about 1/2 minute for over-easy. Place on top of Canadian bacon and English muffin halves and keep warm. Top with Mock Hollandaise Sauce. Makes 2 servings.

**Mock Hollandaise Sauce:**
In a small bowl, combine butter or margarine, mayonnaise and lemon juice. Beat with electric mixer on medium speed to blend well. Makes about 2/3 cup.

**Variation**
To make Cheese-Egg Sandwiches, substitute sliced American cheese for Mock Hollandaise Sauce.

# Huevos Rancheros

*You'll love this Mexican favorite for breakfast, brunch or lunch. Supper, too!*

2 tablespoons vegetable oil
2 (6-inch) corn tortillas
2 eggs
1 tablespoon vegetable oil

1/4 cup chopped onion
1/4 cup chopped green pepper
1/2 cup taco sauce
1/4 cup shredded Cheddar cheese

Prepare unit for open grilling. Add 2 tablespoons of oil to preheated grill. Using tongs, hold tortillas, 1 at a time, and cook in hot oil until crisp, about 1 minute on each side. Remove and keep warm. Break eggs onto grill. Cook until set, 1 to 2 minutes. If desired, turn and continue cooking to desired doneness, about 1/2 minute for over-easy. Place on top of tortillas and keep warm. Add remaining oil to grill. Cook and stir onion and green pepper in oil until tender, about 3 minutes. Stir in taco sauce. Cook and stir until heated through, about 1 minute. Spoon on top of eggs and tortillas. Sprinkle with cheese. Makes 2 servings.

## How to Make Huevos Rancheros

1/Fry tortillas, a side at a time, in hot oil on grill. Next, fry eggs until done to your liking.

2/Spoon the hot taco sauce mixture over the fried eggs. Top with shredded cheese.

# Eggs Florentine

*Who would guess this delicious classic could be so easy?*

1 tablespoon butter or margarine
1 English muffin, halved
1 (12-oz.) pkg. frozen spinach soufflé, thawed

1 tablespoon vegetable oil
2 eggs
2 tablespoons dairy sour cream with chives

Prepare unit for open grilling. On preheated grill, melt 1 tablespoon butter or margarine. Toast muffin halves, cut side down, until light brown, 1/2 to 1 minute. Remove and keep warm. Cook and stir spinach soufflé on grill until heated through, about 2 minutes. Spoon on top of muffin halves and keep warm. Add oil to grill. Break eggs onto grill. Cook until set, about 1 minute. Turn and cook to desired doneness, about 1/2 minute for over-easy. Place on spinach soufflé and muffin halves. Top with sour cream with chives. Makes 2 servings.

# Chicken Egg Foo Young

*You'll crave these delightful Oriental flavors over and over again.*

1/4 cup finely chopped cooked chicken or turkey
2 tablespoons finely chopped celery
2 tablespoons finely chopped green pepper
2 tablespoons finely chopped mushrooms
2 tablespoons finely chopped water chestnuts
1/8 teaspoon salt
Dash pepper

2 eggs, beaten
1 tablespoon vegetable oil
1 tablespoon butter or margarine
2 teaspoons cornstarch
1 teaspoon sugar
1/2 cup water
4 teaspoons soy sauce

Prepare unit for open grilling. In a medium bowl, mix chicken or turkey, celery, green pepper, mushrooms, water chestnuts, salt and pepper. Add eggs; mix well. Add oil to preheated grill. Using 1/4 cup egg mixture for each egg patty, pour onto grill. Cook until brown, about 1 minute on each side. Remove and keep warm. Melt butter or margarine on grill. In a small bowl, mix cornstarch and sugar. Stir into melted butter or margarine on grill. Add water and soy sauce. Cook and stir until mixture thickens, about 2 minutes. Spoon over egg patties. Makes 2 servings.

# Main Dishes

Almost anything you can pan broil or fry, you can cook on your mini-grill. Steaks, from the most expensive sirloin to minute steaks, are delicious right off the grill. You can even grill less tender cuts, as long as you use meat tenderizer. Stir canned gravy or soups into the drippings right on the grill to make a rich sauce. Sprinkle in a few savory herbs and you've created your own mini-grill recipe!

Ground beef appears in many guises. It can be the basis for a fast meal anytime. Try it mixed with frozen vegetables, canned chili or tidbits left from yesterday's dinner. One of my ground beef favorites is Barbecued Meat Loaf. Give it a try.

You'll be rewarded with enthusiastic compliments when you serve Pork Chops Cassis or Sweet & Sour Pork. You can even use sausage and frankfurters to make casserole-type main dishes on your grill. Ham slices, if you buy the fully cooked kind, need only heating through. Veal cutlets, breaded or sautéed in butter, make a very special meal. Or marinate lamb steaks in a spicy sauce or dressing before grilling. Liver cooked in bacon drippings, as in the recipe for Calves Liver Combo, is a nutritious and tasty supper.

Boneless chicken breasts, laid flat on the grill, cook in a few minutes. Batter-fried, breaded or topped with sauce, they make a fabulous entree. Breaded fish sticks and fillets also cook nicely on the grill. And you can even whip up Quick Shrimp Newburg!

# Steak de Burgo

*Burgundy and herbs enhance rib eye steak.*

1 cup Burgundy
1 tablespoon Worcestershire sauce
1/2 teaspoon dried basil
1/2 teaspoon dried thyme
1/4 teaspoon dry mustard

Dash garlic powder
2 (8-oz.) beef rib eye steaks
1/4 cup butter or margarine
4 frozen French-fried onion rings
1/2 cup fresh mushroom slices

In a small bowl, mix Burgundy, Worcestershire sauce, basil, thyme, mustard and garlic powder. Place steaks in a heavy plastic bag. Pour marinade into bag. Seal bag. Marinate in refrigerator 8 hours or overnight, turning steaks occasionally. Prepare unit for open grilling. On preheated grill, melt butter or margarine. Add onion rings. Cook until golden brown, about 1-1/2 minutes on each side. Remove onion rings and keep warm; reserve butter or margarine on grill. Drain steak; reserve 1/2 cup of the marinade. Cook steaks in butter or margarine on grill until done, 8 to 9 minutes for rare, turning several times. Place steaks on a serving platter; reserve drippings on grill. Cook and stir mushrooms in drippings until barely tender, about 1-1/2 minutes. Stir in reserved marinade. Cook and stir until heated through, about 1-1/2 minutes. Pour over steaks. Top with cooked onion rings. Makes 2 servings.

# Mushroom-Smothered Strip Steak

*What could be more appetizing than a juicy steak covered with mushrooms?*

2 tablespoons butter or margarine
2 (8-oz.) New York strip steaks
Salt and pepper to taste

1 tablespoon butter or margarine
1 cup fresh mushroom slices

Prepare unit for open grilling. On preheated grill, melt 2 tablespoons butter or margarine. Add steaks. Cook until done, about 10 minutes for rare, turning several times. Place on a serving platter and keep warm. Season to taste with salt and pepper. Add remaining 1 tablespoon butter or margarine to grill. Add mushrooms. Cook and stir until tender, about 2 minutes. Spoon on top of steaks. Makes 2 servings.

# Jiffy Beef Stroganoff

*Rich and creamy stroganoff becomes a true delicacy served over hot wild rice.*

2 tablespoons butter or margarine
8 oz. beef sirloin steak,
  cut in 1/4-inch strips
1/2 cup fresh mushroom slices
2 tablespoons chopped onion
Garlic salt

1/3 cup beef broth
1 tablespoon all-purpose flour
1 tablespoon ketchup
1/2 cup dairy sour cream
Hot cooked wild rice

Prepare unit for open grilling. On preheated grill, melt butter or margarine. Add steak strips, mushrooms and onion. Cook and stir until almost done, about 3 minutes for rare. Sprinkle with garlic salt. In a small bowl, mix broth, flour and ketchup. Stir into steak and vegetables. Cook and stir until thickened, 1/2 to 1 minute. Place in a medium bowl. Stir in sour cream. Serve immediately over rice. Makes 2 servings.

# Sirloin Tip Roquefort

*Blue cheese salad dressing adds brisk flavor to sliced sirloin rolls.*

1 tablespoon vegetable oil
2 (3-oz.) thin slices beef sirloin tip
Salt and pepper to taste
2 tablespoons blue cheese salad dressing

Boston lettuce leaves
Cherry tomatoes
Crumbled Roquefort or blue cheese

Prepare unit for open grilling. Add oil to preheated grill. Cook steaks 1 at a time in oil until brown, about 1 minute on each side for rare. Season to taste with salt and pepper. Spread sirloin tip slices with dressing. Roll up and secure with wooden picks. Serve on large leaves of lettuce. Garnish with cherry tomatoes and crumbled cheese. Makes 2 servings.

---

*To keep food warm while preparing another dish on the mini-grill, cover with foil—shiny side in. The shiny side will reflect heat back to the food.*

# Hot Reuben Salad

*All the tantalizing flavors of a Reuben sandwich in a hot salad.*

1 tablespoon butter or margarine
1 tablespoon chopped celery
1 tablespoon chopped onion
1 tablespoon chopped green pepper
1 (8-oz.) can sauerkraut,
   drained and rinsed

4 oz. corned beef, cut in strips
1 tablespoon chopped pimiento
1/4 cup Thousand Island dressing
1/2 cup shredded Swiss cheese (2-oz.)
2 rye rolls, if desired

Prepare unit for open grilling. On preheated grill, melt butter or margarine. Add celery, onion and green pepper. Cook and stir until tender, about 3 minutes. Stir in sauerkraut, corned beef, pimiento and dressing. Cook and stir until heated through, about 5 minutes. Top with shredded cheese. Serve with rye rolls, if desired. Makes 2 servings.

# Chinese Pepper Steak

*Serve over rice to temper the exotic Eastern flavor.*

2 tablespoons vegetable oil
1 green pepper, cut in strips
8 oz. beef sirloin steak,
   cut in 1" x 1/8" strips
1 tablespoon water
2 teaspoons cornstarch

1/2 cup beef broth
1 tablespoon soy sauce
1 tablespoon dry sherry
1 garlic clove, minced
1/4 teaspoon grated fresh ginger root

Prepare unit for open grilling. Add oil to preheated grill. Cook and stir green pepper in oil until crisp-tender, about 3 minutes. Remove and keep warm. Add steak strips to grill. Cook and stir until brown, about 5 minutes. Add to green pepper and keep warm; reserve drippings on grill. In a small bowl, mix water and cornstarch; set aside. Stir broth, soy sauce, sherry, garlic and ginger root into drippings on grill. Add cornstarch mixture. Cook and stir until thickened, about 3 minutes. Stir into green pepper and steak. Makes 2 servings.

# Swiss Steak Supper

*A good money-saving recipe.*

8 oz. beef chuck steak, 1/2-inch thick
Unseasoned instant meat tenderizer
1/2 cup all-purpose flour
1/2 teaspoon salt
1/8 teaspoon pepper
2 tablespoons vegetable oil
1 small onion, sliced and separated into rings

1 tablespoon cornstarch
1 cup beef broth
2 tablespoons chili sauce
2 teaspoons brown sugar
1 teaspoon Worcestershire sauce
1 garlic clove, minced

Prepare unit for open grilling. Pound steak with a meat mallet to 1/4-inch thickness. Cut steak in half crosswise. Use meat tenderizer according to package directions. Combine flour, salt and pepper in a plastic bag. Place steak in bag and shake until evenly coated with flour mixture. Add oil to preheated grill. Cook steak in oil until brown, about 7-1/2 minutes. Turn and cook until done, about 7-1/2 minutes for rare. Place on a platter and keep warm; reserve drippings on grill. Cook and stir onion rings in drippings until tender, about 4 minutes. Stir cornstarch into onions and drippings on grill. Add broth, chili sauce, brown sugar, Worcestershire sauce and garlic. Cook and stir until thickened, about 2 minutes. Spoon over steaks. Makes 2 servings.

# Calves Liver Combo

*Cook liver a little on the rare side. Overcooked liver is tough and dry.*

3 slices bacon
1/2 onion, sliced and separated into rings
1/2 cup all-purpose flour
1/2 teaspoon salt
1/8 teaspoon pepper

8 oz. calves liver
2 tablespoons vegetable oil
1 teaspoon all-purpose flour
1/2 cup beef broth

Prepare unit for open grilling. On preheated grill, cook bacon until crisp, 3 to 4 minutes. Crumble bacon and set aside; reserve drippings on grill. Cook onion in drippings until tender, about 4 minutes. Add to bacon. In a pie plate, mix 1/2 cup flour, salt and pepper. Dredge liver in flour mixture. Add oil to grill. Cook and turn liver in oil until done, about 5 minutes. Remove and keep warm; reserve drippings on grill. Stir 1 teaspoon flour into drippings. Stir in beef broth, crumbled bacon and cooked onion. Cook and stir until thickened, about 2 minutes. Spoon over liver. Makes 2 servings.

# Barbecued Meat Loaf

*This mini meat loaf is packed with true barbecue flavor.*

12 oz. ground beef
1 egg, beaten
1/3 cup barbecue sauce
1/4 cup cheese cracker crumbs
1 tablespoon dehydrated minced onion flakes

1 tablespoon dehydrated green pepper flakes
1/2 teaspoon celery salt
Vegetable oil
1/4 cup barbecue sauce
1/2 cup shredded process American cheese

Prepare unit for closed grilling. In a medium bowl, mix ground beef, egg, 1/3 cup barbecue sauce, cracker crumbs, onion flakes, green pepper flakes and celery salt. Brush both sides of grill with oil. Pat ground beef mixture onto bottom half of preheated grill. Close grill, but do not latch. Cook until brown, about 4 minutes. Using 2 spatulas, turn carefully. If necessary, pat back into shape after turning. Cook until done, about 3 minutes. To remove meat loaf from grill, place serving plate on top of loaf and flip grill tray. Top with remaining barbecue sauce and cheese. Makes 3 to 4 servings.

# Gourmet Beef & Macaroni

*Ground beef, mushrooms and a few extras turn macaroni and cheese into a gourmet's delight.*

8 oz. ground beef
1 (2-1/2-oz.) can sliced mushrooms, drained
3 tablespoons chopped pimiento
1/4 teaspoon dried thyme
4 slices tomato

Seasoned salt
1 (12-oz.) pkg. frozen macaroni and cheese, thawed
Snipped fresh parsley

Prepare unit for open grilling. On preheated grill, cook and stir ground beef, mushrooms, pimiento and thyme until meat is brown, about 6 minutes. Place in a medium serving bowl and keep warm. Grill tomato slices until heated through, about 1 minute on each side. Sprinkle with seasoned salt. Remove and keep warm. Cook and stir macaroni on grill until heated through, about 2 minutes. Stir macaroni into beef. Top with tomato slices and sprinkle with snipped parsley. Makes 3 servings.

---

*Eggs should be slightly beaten when used for thickening. To avoid curdling, stir a moderate amount of hot mixture into eggs before adding to remaining hot mixture. Cook and stir mixture until thickened and bubbly.*

# Swedish-Style Meatballs

*These hearty meatballs are perfect over egg noodles.*

4 oz. ground beef
4 oz. ground pork
1 egg, beaten
1 cup soft breadcrumbs (3 slices bread)
1/4 cup chopped onion
1/4 cup milk
1/2 teaspoon salt

1/8 teaspoon ground nutmeg
1/8 teaspoon pepper
2 tablespoons butter or margarine
2 tablespoons all-purpose flour
1 cup milk
1/8 teaspoon ground nutmeg
Salt and pepper to taste

Prepare unit for open grilling. In a medium bowl, mix beef, pork, egg, breadcrumbs, onion, 1/4 cup milk, salt, 1/8 teaspoon nutmeg and pepper. Shape into twelve 1-inch balls. On preheated grill, melt butter or margarine. Add meatballs, 6 at a time. Cook, turning frequently until done, about 5 to 6 minutes. Remove and keep warm; reserve drippings on grill. Stir flour into drippings. Add remaining milk and nutmeg. Cook and stir until thickened, about 1 minute. Season to taste with salt and pepper. Pour over meatballs. Makes 3 to 4 servings.

## How to Make Swedish-Style Meatballs

1/With wet hands, lightly shape the ground pork and beef mixture into balls.

2/Cook meatballs in butter or margarine, turning often so all sides will cook evenly.

# Chunky Chili With Cheese

*To make extra-juicy chili, stir in 1/4 cup of tomato juice.*

8 oz. ground beef
4 oz. process American cheese,
   cut in 1/2-inch cubes (1 cup)
1 (8-oz.) can red kidney beans, drained

1 (8-oz.) can tomatoes, chopped
1 tablespoon dehydrated minced onion flakes
1 teaspoon garlic salt
1 teaspoon chili powder

Prepare unit for open grilling. On preheated grill, cook and stir ground beef until done, 3 to 4 minutes. Remove; stir in cheese and keep warm. Drain drippings from grill. Combine beans, tomatoes, onion flakes, garlic salt and chili powder on grill. Cook and stir until heated through, 2 to 3 minutes. Stir into ground beef mixture. Makes 2 servings.

# Pork Chops With Apple Stuffing

*Succulent chops with an unusual apple-raisin-bread stuffing.*

1 tablespoon vegetable oil
2 (4-oz.) pork loin chops, 1/2-inch thick
1/4 cup chopped apple
1/4 cup chopped celery

3 slices raisin bread, cubed
3 tablespoons apple juice
Dash ground nutmeg

Prepare unit for open grilling. Add oil to preheated grill. Cook pork chops in oil until brown, about 5 minutes on each side. Remove and keep warm; reserve 2 tablespoons drippings on grill. Cook and stir apple and celery in drippings until tender, about 2 minutes. In a small bowl, mix raisin bread, apple juice and nutmeg. Add to apple and celery mixture. Cook and stir until heated through, about 2 minutes. Serve with pork chops. Makes 2 servings.

---

*If chopping fresh onions leaves you in tears, substitute dehydrated minced onion flakes. Rehydrate in water before using in a recipe low in liquid. One tablespoon dehydrated flakes is equivalent to about 1 small fresh onion.*

# Sweet & Sour Pork

*If you stay home and cook this, you won't mind not going out for Chinese food.*

1/4 cup dry sherry
2 tablespoons soy sauce
1 tablespoon red wine vinegar
8 oz. boneless pork, cut in 1-inch cubes
1 egg, beaten

1/4 cup all-purpose flour
1/4 cup cornstarch
1/3 cup vegetable oil
Sweet & Sour Sauce, see below

*Sweet & Sour Sauce:*
1/2 cup tomato sauce
1/4 cup brown sugar, firmly packed
1/4 cup red wine vinegar
1/4 cup pineapple juice
2 tablespoons cornstarch

2 tablespoons cold water
1/2 cup pineapple chunks
1/4 cup coarsely chopped onion
1/4 cup coarsely chopped green pepper

In a small bowl, mix sherry, soy sauce and 1 tablespoon vinegar. Pour over pork cubes. Marinate 10 minutes at room temperature. In a small bowl, mix egg, flour and 1/4 cup cornstarch. Drain pork and dip in flour mixture, making sure each piece is coated evenly. Prepare unit for open grilling. Add oil to preheated grill. Cook pork in hot oil until done, about 7 minutes, turning often. Remove pork and keep warm.

**Sweet & Sour Sauce:**
Prepare unit for open grilling. In a small bowl, mix tomato sauce, brown sugar, vinegar and pineapple juice. Cook and stir on preheated grill until heated through, about 1 minute. In a small bowl or cup, stir 2 tablespoons cornstarch into water. Add to tomato mixture. Stir in pineapple, onion and green pepper. Cook and stir until thickened, about 3 minutes. Spoon over pork cubes. Makes 2 servings.

# Smoked Pork Chops Cassis

*Creme de cassis is a sweet liqueur made from black currants.*

1/4 cup black currant jelly
1 tablespoon crème de cassis

1 tablespoon vegetable oil
2 (4-oz.) smoked pork chops, 1/2-inch thick

Prepare unit for open grilling. In a small bowl, mix jelly and crème de cassis. Set aside. Add oil to preheated grill. Cook pork chops until light brown, about 4 minutes. Turn, spoon glaze on chops, and cook until other side is light brown and heated through, about 4 minutes. Spoon glaze over chops several times during last 4 minutes of cooking to prevent glaze from burning. Makes 2 servings.

# Brandied Fruit Pork Chops

*Fruit and brandy add elegance to grilled pork chops.*

1 tablespoon vegetable oil
2 (6-oz.) pork loin chops, 1/2-inch thick
Salt and pepper to taste
1/3 cup peach slices
1/3 cup pineapple chunks

1/3 cup orange marmalade
1 tablespoon brandy
2 slices orange
2 slices lime
2 maraschino cherries, if desired

Prepare unit for open grilling. Add oil to preheated grill. Cook pork chops in oil until brown, about 5 minutes on each side. Season to taste with salt and pepper. Remove and keep warm. Drain drippings from grill. Combine peaches, pineapple, marmalade and brandy on grill. Cook and stir until heated through, about 2 minutes. Spoon over chips. Top with orange slices, lime slices and maraschino cherries, if desired. Makes 2 servings.

# Pork Wild Rice Supper

*Thaw rice quickly under running water while vegetables and pork are cooking.*

2 tablespoons vegetable oil
1 (2-1/2-oz.) can mushrooms, drained
3 tablespoons chopped green onion
2 (4-oz.) pork tenderloins, cut in 1-inch strips

1 (11-oz.) pkg. frozen long grain and
  wild rice, thawed
1 tomato, cubed

Prepare unit for open grilling. Add oil to preheated grill. Cook mushrooms and onion in oil until tender, about 3 minutes. Remove and keep warm. Add pork strips to grill; cook and stir until done, about 5 minutes. Combine with mushrooms and onion, keep warm. Cook rice and tomato on grill until heated through, about 4 minutes. Stir into pork mixture. Makes 3 servings.

*The mini-grill is ideal for quick sautéing fresh mushroom slices. On preheated open grill, melt about 2 tablespoons butter or margarine. Add mushrooms. Cook and stir until tender. One cup takes about 1-1/2 minutes. One-half cup takes about 1/2 to 1 minute.*

# Hot Sausage Supper, German-Style

*Sausage and potatoes nestled in a tangy sauce.*

8 oz. smoked sausage,
  cut in 1-inch pieces
3 slices bacon
1/4 cup chopped onion
1/4 cup chopped green pepper
1 tablespoon all-purpose flour
1 tablespoon sugar

1/2 teaspoon dry mustard
1/2 teaspoon celery seed
1/2 teaspoon salt
1/2 cup water
1/4 cup cider vinegar
1 (8-oz.) can whole potatoes,
  drained and sliced

Prepare unit for open grilling. On preheated grill, cook sausage, turning often, until heated through, about 2 minutes. Remove and keep warm. Cook bacon on grill until crisp, 3 to 4 minutes. Crumble bacon and set aside; reserve drippings on grill. Cook and stir onion and green pepper in drippings until tender, about 2 minutes. Stir in flour, sugar, mustard, celery seed and salt. Add water and vinegar. Cook and stir until thickened, about 2-1/2 minutes. Stir in potatoes. Cook and stir until heated through, about 2 minutes. Add to sausage. Top with bacon. Makes 2 to 3 servings.

# Chuck Wagon Supper

*Great served in tin plates around a campfire or at your own table.*

3 slices bacon
3 frankfurters, cut in 1-inch pieces
1 (8-oz.) can pork 'n beans
2 tablespoons chopped onion

2 tablespoons ketchup
2 teaspoons brown sugar
2 teaspoons prepared mustard

Prepare unit for open grilling. On preheated grill, cook bacon until crisp, 3 to 4 minutes. Crumble bacon and set aside; reserve drippings on grill. Add frankfurter pieces to grill. Cook and turn until heated through, about 2 minutes. Place in a medium bowl and keep warm. Combine pork 'n beans, onion, ketchup, brown sugar, mustard and reserved bacon on grill. Cook and stir until heated through, about 2 minutes. Stir in frankfurters. Makes 2 servings.

# Ham Yam Logs

*Everyone goes bananas over these ham roll-ups with sweet potato and fruit filling.*

| | |
|---|---|
| 1 (8-oz.) can sweet potatoes, drained | Brown sugar |
| 1 medium banana, sliced | Ground cinnamon |
| 1/4 cup pineapple preserves | 1 tablespoon butter or margarine |
| 4 large thin slices cooked ham | Cranberry-orange relish for garnish |

Prepare unit for open grilling. In a medium bowl, mix sweet potatoes, banana and pineapple preserves. Spoon onto each ham slice. Sprinkle with brown sugar and cinnamon. Roll up and secure with wooden picks. On preheated grill, melt butter or margarine. Add roll-ups. Cook until heated through, 2-1/2 to 3 minutes, turning often. Garnish with cranberry-orange relish. Makes 4 servings.

# Pineapple Ham Loaf

*Ham and pork loaf with a tropical glaze.*

| | |
|---|---|
| 8 oz. ground ham | 1/4 cup quick-cooking oats |
| 4 oz. ground pork | 1/4 cup ketchup |
| 1 egg, beaten | Vegetable oil |
| 1/4 cup chopped onion | Pineapple Glaze, see below |

*Pineapple Glaze:*

| | |
|---|---|
| 1 tablespoon butter or margarine | 2 canned pineapple slices, halved |
| 2 tablespoons brown sugar | |

Prepare unit for closed grilling. In a medium bowl, mix ham, pork, egg, onion, oats and ketchup. Mix well. Brush both sides of preheated grill with oil. Pat ham mixture onto bottom half of grill. Close lid, but do not latch. Cook until brown, 5 to 6 minutes. Using 2 spatulas, turn carefully. If necessary, pat back into shape after turning. Cook until done, 3 to 4 minutes. To remove ham loaf from grill, place serving plate on top of loaf and flip grill tray. Prepare Pineapple Glaze. Spoon over ham loaf. Makes 4 servings.

**Pineapple Glaze:**
Prepare unit for open grilling. On preheated grill, melt butter or margarine. Stir in brown sugar. Add pineapple and cook until heated through, about 1 minute on each side. Makes about 1/4 cup.

# Veal Cordon Bleu á la Ascona

*A delicious variation of the popular classic—ham and Swiss cheese between tender veal slices.*

2 (4-oz.) veal sirloin steaks
2 slices cooked ham
2 slices Swiss cheese
Dash ground sage

2 tablespoons butter or margarine
1 cup fresh mushroom slices
1/4 cup dry white wine

Prepare unit for open grilling. Pound veal steaks with a meat mallet to 1/8-inch thickness. Cut in half crosswise. Place a ham slice, then a cheese slice on 2 of the halves. Sprinkle with sage. Top with second veal steak halves. Pound edges to seal. On preheated grill, melt butter or margarine. Cook veal until brown, about 4 minutes on each side. Place on a serving platter; reserve drippings on grill. Cook and stir mushrooms in drippings until tender, about 1-1/2 minutes. Stir in wine. Cook and stir until heated through, about 1/2 minute. Spoon over veal. Makes 2 servings.

## How to Make Veal Cordon Bleu á la Ascona

1/Pound veal until it is 1/8-inch thick. Halve the veal steak crosswise. Top 1 half with a slice of ham and a slice of cheese.

2/Place the second half of veal over the ham and cheese slices, then pound the edges with a meat mallet to seal.

# Veal Scallopini

*If veal sirloin steaks are not available, use veal loin or rib chops, round steaks or shoulder steaks.*

2 (4-oz.) boneless veal sirloin steaks
Salt and pepper to taste
2 tablespoons butter or margarine
1/2 cup chopped onion

1/2 cup chopped mushrooms
1/4 cup beef broth
1 tablespoon dry sherry

Prepare unit for open grilling. Pound veal with a meat mallet to 1/8-inch thickness. Sprinkle with salt and pepper. On preheated grill, melt butter or margarine. Add onion and mushrooms. Cook and stir until tender, about 2 minutes. Place on a platter and keep warm. Cook veal on grill until brown and done, 1-1/2 to 2-1/2 minutes on each side. Add to onion and mushrooms on platter; keep warm. Cook and stir broth and sherry on grill until heated through, about 1/2 minute. Spoon over onion, mushrooms and veal. Makes 2 servings.

# Quick Veal Parmigiana

*You'll love this zesty meal when you get a craving for Italian food.*

2 (4-oz.) veal sirloin steaks
3/4 cup seasoned breadcrumbs
1/4 cup grated Parmesan cheese
1 egg, beaten

1/4 cup vegetable oil
1 cup Italian cooking sauce
1/4 cup shredded mozzarella cheese

Prepare unit for open grilling. Pound veal with a meat mallet to 1/8-inch thickness. In a pie plate, mix breadcrumbs and Parmesan cheese. Dip veal in crumb mixture, then in egg, then again in crumb mixture. Add oil to preheated grill. Cook breaded veal in hot oil until brown and done, about 3 minutes on each side. Place on a platter and keep warm. Drain drippings from grill. Cook and stir Italian sauce on grill until heated through, about 1-1/2 minutes. Spoon over veal and sprinkle with mozzarella cheese. Makes 2 servings.

*Suggested seasonings for veal are: basil, bay leaf, chervil, dill, fennel, garlic, oregano, parsley, rosemary, sage, tansy and thyme.*

# Zeus' Lamb Steaks

*Greek-style lamb—food for the gods!*

2 (8-oz.) lamb blade steaks, 1/2-inch thick
Garlic salt to taste
Dried oregano to taste
Dried basil to taste

Pepper to taste
1 tablespoon olive oil
2 lemon wedges

Prepare unit for open grilling. Sprinkle lamb with garlic salt, oregano, basil and pepper. Add olive oil to preheated grill. Cook lamb in oil until brown and done, 2-1/2 to 3 minutes on each side for medium. Serve with lemon wedges. Makes 2 servings.

# Cacciatore Chicken Breasts

Cacciatore *means hunter's style—simmered in wine with onions, tomatoes, garlic and herbs.*

2 tablespoons olive oil
1/2 onion, sliced and separated into rings
1/2 green pepper, sliced
2 chicken breasts, skinned,
   boned and halved

1 (8-oz.) can stewed tomatoes
2 tablespoons dry white wine
1/2 teaspoon garlic salt
1/4 teaspoon dried rosemary
1/8 teaspoon pepper

Prepare unit for open grilling. Add olive oil to preheated grill. Cook and stir onion and green pepper in oil until tender, about 6 minutes. Remove and keep warm. Cook chicken on grill until brown and done, about 3-1/2 to 4 minutes on each side. Remove and keep warm. Combine tomatoes, wine, garlic salt, rosemary and pepper on grill. Cook and stir until heated through, about 3 minutes. Stir in onion and green pepper. Serve over chicken. Makes 2 servings.

# Hot Garbanzo Chicken Salad

*A nifty quick-and-easy luncheon.*

3 slices bacon
1/4 cup almonds
1 (15-oz.) can garbanzo beans,
   drained and rinsed
1 (5-oz.) can boned chicken

1/4 cup chopped green onion
2 tablespoons chopped pimiento
1/4 cup Italian salad dressing
2 oz. Monterey Jack cheese,
   cut in 1/2-inch cubes (1/2 cup)

Prepare unit for open grilling. On preheated grill, cook bacon until crisp, 3 to 4 minutes. Crumble bacon and set aside; reserve drippings on grill. Cook almonds in drippings until toasted, about 1 minute. Add to bacon; reserve drippings on grill. Add garbanzos, chicken, onion, pimiento and dressing to drippings. Cook and stir until heated through, about 4 minutes. Spoon into a serving bowl. Add cheese cubes, crumbled bacon and almonds; toss lightly. Makes 4 servings.

# Easy Chicken a la King

*You can make it at a moment's notice!*

2 tablespoons butter or margarine
1 (5-oz.) can boned chicken
1 (2-1/2-oz.) can mushrooms, drained
1 (10-1/4-oz.) can condensed
   cream of mushroom soup

1/4 cup milk
2 tablespoons chopped pimiento
2 tablespoons dry white wine
2 English muffins, halved

Prepare unit for open grilling. On preheated grill, melt butter or margarine. Add chicken and mushrooms. Cook and stir until heated through, about 3 minutes. Place in a medium bowl and keep warm. Combine soup, milk, pimiento and wine on grill. Cook and stir until heated through, about 2 minutes. Stir into chicken and mushrooms. Serve over English muffin halves. Makes 4 servings.

---

*To avoid lumps in sauces and gravies, blend flour or cornstarch with fat, sugar or cold liquid before combining with a hot mixture. Cook and stir until mixture thickens and bubbles.*

# Chicken Veronique Supreme

*Fresh green grapes and dry white wine enhance chicken breasts sautéed in lemon and butter.*

1/2 lemon
2 (4-oz.) chicken breasts, skinned,
   boned and halved
Salt and pepper to taste
2 tablespoons butter or margarine

1 tablespoon cold water
1 teaspoon cornstarch
1/2 cup seedless green grapes
1/3 cup light cream
1 tablespoon dry white wine

Prepare unit for open grilling. Squeeze lemon juice over chicken. Sprinkle with salt and pepper. On preheated grill, melt butter or margarine. Add chicken breasts. Cook until brown and done, 3-1/2 to 4 minutes on each side. Remove and keep warm; reserve drippings on grill. In a small bowl, mix water and cornstarch. Stir into drippings on grill. Add grapes and cream. Cook and stir until sauce thickens, about 2-1/2 minutes. Stir in wine. Spoon sauce over chicken.

## How to Make Chicken Veronique Supreme

**1/Bone and skin 2 chicken breasts. Squeeze lemon juice over chicken and sprinkle with salt and pepper.**

**2/Cook chicken in butter or margarine until tender. Top with a classic creamy wine and green grape sauce.**

# Orange-Glazed Drumsticks

*Chicken and oranges make an intriguing pair.*

2 tablespoons vegetable oil
4 chicken drumsticks
Salt and pepper to taste
1/4 cup water
2 tablespoons orange juice concentrate

1 tablespoon brown sugar
1/2 teaspoon prepared mustard
1 (11-oz.) can mandarin orange sections,
   drained
1 cup cooked rice, if desired

Prepare unit for open grilling. Add oil to preheated grill. Sprinkle chicken with salt and pepper. Cook and turn chicken in hot oil until done, about 35 minutes. Drain drippings from grill. In a small bowl, mix water, orange juice concentrate, brown sugar and mustard. Add to chicken on grill. Cook and turn chicken in glaze until glaze thickens and chicken is coated, about 4 minutes. Stir in orange sections. Cook and stir until heated through, about 2 minutes. Serve over rice, if desired. Makes 2 servings.

# Grilled Turkey Birds

*Turkey rolls stuffed with a unique sausage and spinach dressing.*

4 oz. bulk pork sausage
1 tablespoon chopped onion
1/2 (8-oz.) can spinach, drained and chopped
1/4 cup herb-seasoned breadcrumbs
   for stuffing

1 tablespoon grated Parmesan cheese
4 large thin slices turkey
2 tablespoons butter or margarine
1/2 teaspoon dried sage

Prepare unit for open grilling. On preheated grill, cook and stir sausage and onion until sausage is done, about 4 minutes. Stir in spinach, breadcrumbs and Parmesan cheese. Cook and stir until heated through, about 1 minute. Spoon sausage stuffing onto turkey slices. Roll up and secure with wooden picks. Melt butter or margarine on grill. Stir in sage. Add turkey roll-ups. Cook until heated through, about 2 minutes, turning occasionally. Makes 4 servings.

---

*To test chicken for doneness, pierce close to the bone with a fork or knife. Chicken is usually done when no pink color remains in the juice.*

---

# Crab Norfolk

*Although nothing beats fresh crabmeat, frozen crabmeat is available year-round!*

6 oz. fresh or thawed frozen crabmeat, flaked
2 tablespoons chopped green onion
1 teaspoon white wine vinegar

1/8 teaspoon salt
Dash cayenne pepper
2 tablespoons butter or margarine

Prepare unit for open grilling. In a medium bowl, mix crabmeat, onion, vinegar, salt and cayenne pepper. On preheated grill, melt butter or margarine. Add crabmeat mixture. Cook and stir until heated through, about 4 minutes. Makes 2 servings.

# Deviled Crab Cakes

*So good your guest will ask for seconds!*

8 oz. fresh or thawed frozen crabmeat, flaked
1 cup soft breadcrumbs (3 slices)
1 egg, beaten
1 tablespoon mayonnaise
1 teaspoon snipped fresh parsley

1/2 teaspoon prepared mustard
1/4 teaspoon dried thyme
1/8 teaspoon dried sage
Vegetable oil
4 lemon wedges

Prepare unit for closed grilling. In a medium bowl, mix crabmeat, breadcrumbs, egg, mayonnaise, parsley, mustard, thyme and sage. Shape into 4 patties. Brush both sides of preheated grill with oil. Place 2 patties on grill. Close cover, but do not latch. Cook until brown and done, about 1 minute on each side. Repeat with remaining patties. Serve with lemon wedges. Makes 4 servings.

# Quick Shrimp Newburg

*Convenience foods can shorten the preparation of this gourmet meal from hours to minutes.*

2 tablespoons butter or margarine

8 oz. cooked shrimp, peeled and deveined

2 tablespoons chopped green onion

2 tablespoons chopped celery

Dash garlic powder

1 (10-oz.) pkg. frozen Welsh rarebit, thawed

2 tablespoons dry sherry

2 to 3 baked patty shells

2 tablespoons grated Parmesan cheese

Snipped fresh dillweed for garnish

Prepare unit for open grilling. On preheated grill, melt butter or margarine. Add shrimp, onion and celery. Cook and stir until shrimp is heated through and vegetables are tender, about 4 minutes. Sprinkle with garlic powder. Stir rarebit and sherry into shrimp mixture. Cook and stir until heated through, about 3 minutes. Spoon into patty shells. Sprinkle with parmesan cheese and dillweed. Makes 2 to 3 servings.

# Mexican Chili & Beans

*If you aren't a green chili enthusiast, substitute more chopped onion for the chilies.*

2 (6-inch) corn tortillas

1/2 cup refried beans

2 tablespoons canned chopped green chilies

1 tablespoon chopped onion

1/4 cup shredded Monterey Jack cheese (1-oz.)

Vegetable oil

Taco Sauce

Prepare unit for open grilling. Spread half of each tortilla with beans. Top with chilies, onion and cheese. Fold tortillas over, forming a half-moon shape. Brush both sides of tortillas lightly with oil. Cook on preheated grill until light brown, 2 to 2-1/2 minutes on each side. Serve with taco sauce. Makes 2 servings.

# *Vegetables*

Keep your mini-grill handy for stir-frying fresh vegetables. Use small quantities at a time, and cut the vegetables to uniform thickness to ensure even cooking. The finishing touch is a few herbs sprinkled over the top. To get started, try the Stir-Fry Vegetable Medley.

Thawed frozen vegetables can be the basis for lots of easy and interesting ideas. Just add water to one of the many frozen vegetable mixtures on the market and cook according to package directions. Try sautéing a little onion and a few herbs in butter before adding the vegetables. You'll discover a neat trick with maple syrup when you try Maple-Glazed Carrots.

All the frozen potato products that require shallow frying can be cooked successfully on your mini-grill.

For an appealing and wholesome appetizer or snack, pass a plateful of Battered Vegetables. They make an unusual and nutritious change from the chip-and-dip routine.

Instead of tossing your regular salad tonight, try a hot spinach or wilted lettuce salad. Cook bacon on the mini-grill, add onion to the drippings and stir in a little vinegar, sugar and a dash of water. Look at the complete recipe for Wilted Spinach Salad in this section for more precise directions. You'll be glad you did.

# Wilted Spinach Salad

*For variety, substitute your favorite fresh lettuce for the spinach or add sautéed mushrooms.*

4 slices bacon
2 tablespoons chopped green onion
1/4 cup red wine vinegar
2 tablespoons water
1 teaspoon sugar
1 teaspoon Worcestershire sauce

1/2 teaspoon dry mustard
1/4 teaspoon salt
Dash pepper
1/2 (10-oz.) pkg. fresh spinach
2 hard-boiled eggs, sliced
1 tomato, peeled and quartered

Prepare unit for open grilling. On preheated grill, cook bacon until crisp, 4 to 5 minutes. Remove bacon; reserve drippings on grill. Crumble bacon and set aside. Cook and stir onion in drippings until tender, about 2 minutes. Stir in vinegar, water, sugar, Worcestershire, mustard, salt, pepper and reserved bacon. Bring to boiling, about 1 minute, stirring occasionally. In a salad bowl, mix spinach, eggs and tomato. Pour dressing over salad and toss. Makes 4 servings.

# Herb-Fried Tomatoes

*To be suitable for frying, tomatoes should be either green and mature or red and firm.*

1 large, firm tomato, sliced 1/4-inch thick
Salt and pepper to taste
1 cup herb-seasoned breadcrumbs for stuffing,
   finely crushed

1 egg, beaten
2 tablespoons vegetable oil
Shredded Cheddar cheese

Prepare unit for open grilling. Sprinkle tomato slices with salt and pepper. Place breadcrumbs and egg in 2 separate pie plates. Dip tomato slices in breadcrumbs, then in egg, then again in breadcrumbs. Add oil to preheated grill. Cook tomato slices in hot oil until golden brown, 1-1/2 minutes on each side. Top with shredded Cheddar cheese. Makes 2 servings.

# Eggplant Parmigiana Stack-Ups

*Use as a main dish or serve with your next spaghetti dinner.*

1 cup seasoned breadcrumbs
2 eggs, beaten
1 eggplant, sliced 1/2-inch thick (12 slices)
6 tablespoons vegetable oil

6 slices mozzarella cheese, halved
1/2 (21-oz.) jar Italian cooking sauce
1/2 cup grated Parmesan cheese

Prepare unit for open grilling. Place breadcrumbs and eggs in 2 separate pie plates. Dip eggplant slices in breadcrumbs, then in egg, then again in crumbs. Add 1 tablespoon oil to preheated grill. Cook eggplant slices, 2 at a time, in hot oil until golden brown, about 2-1/2 minutes on each side. Drain. Top each eggplant slice with a half slice of cheese. Repeat with remaining oil, eggplant and half slices of cheese. Remove from grill; keep warm. Add Italian cooking sauce to grill. Cook and stir until heated through, about 3 minutes. Spoon over half the eggplant and cheese slices. Sprinkle with half the Parmesan cheese. Cover with remaining eggplant and cheese slices. Top with remaining sauce and Parmesan cheese. Makes 6 stack-ups.

## How to Make Eggplant Parmigiana Stack-Ups

1/Cook the breaded eggplant slices until golden brown, then turn and top with a slice of mozzarella cheese. Add more oil to the grill while cooking, if necessary.

2/Heat the ready-made Italian cooking sauce on the grill. Spoon the sauce between eggplant layers and over the top of the stack. Pass Parmesan cheese to sprinkle over the top.

# Battered Vegetables

*Kids love these. Dish up a bowlful for snacking or to go with dinner.*

1/2 cup cornmeal
1/2 cup all-purpose flour
1/2 teaspoon salt
1/8 teaspoon paprika
1/8 teaspoon pepper
1 egg
1 tablespoon water

2 cups assorted vegetables:
   cauliflowerets; broccoli flowerets;
   mushrooms; carrots, summer squash, *or*
   zucchini, cut in diagonal 1/4-inch slices
1/3 cup vegetable oil
Salt and pepper to taste

Prepare unit for open grilling. In a pie plate, mix cornmeal, flour, 1/2 teaspoon salt, paprika and 1/8 teaspoon pepper. In another pie plate, mix egg and water. Dip vegetables in cornmeal-flour mixture, then in egg, then again in cornmeal-flour mixture. Add oil to preheated grill. Cook vegetables, 1 cup at a time, in hot oil until crisp-tender and golden brown, about 3 minutes, turning occasionally. Season to taste with salt and pepper. Repeat with remaining vegetables. Makes 3 to 4 servings.

# Elegant Green Beans

*The cream cheese topping is also a success with broccoli and asparagus—try it!*

3 slices bacon
1 (16-oz.) can green beans
1 (3-oz.) pkg. cream cheese, softened

1 tablespoon water
1/2 teaspoon dried dillweed

Prepare unit for open grilling. On preheated grill, cook bacon until crisp, 3 to 4 minutes. Remove bacon; reserve drippings on grill. Crumble bacon and set aside. Drain beans; reserve 1/4 cup liquid. Add liquid to drippings on grill. Add beans. Cook until heated through, about 4 minutes. In a small bowl, mix bacon, cream cheese, water and dillweed. Stir until no cream cheese lumps remain. Spoon over green beans. Makes 3 servings.

*To make carrot curls, slice a peeled carrot in half lengthwise and cut in long thin strips. Roll up each strip and secure with a wooden pick. Store in cold water in the refrigerator.*

# Stir-Fry Vegetable Medley

*Fresh ginger root puts zip in crisp garden vegetables.*

1 tablespoon vegetable oil
1 small yellow summer squash, thinly sliced
1/2 small red or green pepper, cut in strips
3 cauliflowerets, thinly sliced
1 carrot, thinly sliced

2 green onions, sliced
1/2 teaspoon garlic salt
1/2 teaspoon grated fresh ginger root
1 tablespoon snipped fresh parsley or tarragon

Prepare unit for open grilling. Add oil to preheated grill. Add squash, pepper, cauliflowerets, carrot and green onions. Sprinkle with garlic salt and ginger root. Cook and stir until vegetables are crisp-tender, about 7 minutes. Spoon onto serving plate and sprinkle with parsley or tarragon. Makes 3 servings.

# Hot German Potato Salad

*This tangy potato salad goes great with sandwiches or burgers.*

2 tablespoons vegetable oil
1 (16-oz.) can potatoes,
    sliced 1/4-inch thick
2 tablespoons chopped pimiento
3 slices bacon
1/2 cup chopped onion
2 teaspoons all-purpose flour

1/2 cup water
2 tablespoons cider vinegar
4 teaspoons sugar
1 tablespoon snipped fresh parsley
1/4 teaspoon salt
Parsley for garnish, if desired

Prepare unit for open grilling. Add oil to preheated grill. Cook and stir potatoes and pimiento until heated through, about 4 minutes. Remove and keep warm. Cook bacon until crisp, 3 to 4 minutes. Remove bacon; reserve drippings on grill. Crumble bacon and add to potatoes. Cook and stir onion in bacon drippings until tender, about 3 minutes. Stir in flour. Add water, vinegar, sugar, 1 tablespoon parsley and salt. Cook and stir until mixture thickens, about 2 minutes. Pour over potatoes and bacon. Toss gently. Garnish with additional parsley, if desired. Makes 2 to 3 servings.

# Hashed Browns O'Brien

*If you have them on hand, you can substitute sliced or grated canned potato.*

1 medium, raw potato
1/4 cup chopped onion
1/4 cup chopped green pepper
2 tablespoons chopped pimiento

1/4 teaspoon salt
Dash pepper
2 tablespoons vegetable oil

Prepare unit for open grilling. Grate potato into a small bowl. Stir in onion, green pepper, pimiento, salt and pepper. Mix well. Add oil to preheated grill. Pat potato mixture onto grill. Cook until bottom side is golden brown, about 5 minutes. Cut potato mixture in half and turn, a half at a time. Cook until other side is golden brown, about another 5 minutes. Makes 2 servings.

# Sweet & Sour Red Cabbage

*Red wine vinegar and brown sugar add a piquant flavor to red cabbage.*

2 tablespoons butter or margarine
3/4 cup chopped red cabbage
3/4 cup chopped apple
1/4 cup water

2 tablespoons red wine vinegar
1 tablespoon brown sugar
1/2 teaspoon caraway seed
Salt and pepper to taste

Prepare unit for open grilling. On preheated grill, melt butter or margarine. Add cabbage and apple. Cook and stir until crisp-tender, about 4 minutes. In a small bowl, mix water, vinegar, brown sugar and caraway seed. Stir into cabbage-apple mixture on grill. Cook and stir until heated through, about 1/2 minute. Season to taste with salt and pepper. Makes 3 servings.

# Maple-Glazed Carrots

*Buttery maple syrup makes sweet and tender carrots a real delicacy.*

1-1/4 cups frozen carrots, thawed
3/4 cup water
3 tablespoons butter or margarine

3 tablespoons maple syrup
1/2 teaspoon grated lemon peel
1/8 teaspoon ground mace

Prepare unit for open grilling. Add carrots and water to preheated grill. Cook and stir until crisp-tender, about 8 minutes. Add butter or margarine to carrots on grill. In a small bowl or cup, mix maple syrup, lemon peel and mace. Pour over carrots on grill. Cook and stir until carrots are lightly glazed, about 2 minutes. Makes 2 to 3 servings.

# Vegetarian Fried Rice

*Enjoy this with your most exotic Oriental dish.*

2 tablespoons vegetable oil
1/4 cup bean sprouts
2 tablespoons chopped green onion
2 tablespoons chopped green or red pepper
2 tablespoons chopped celery

1/8 teaspoon garlic salt
1/4 cup water
1 teaspoon soy sauce
1/2 (12-oz.) can fried rice

Prepare unit for open grilling. Add oil to preheated grill. Add bean sprouts, onion, pepper and celery. Cook and stir until crisp-tender, about 3 minutes. Sprinkle with garlic salt. Remove and keep warm. Add water and soy sauce to grill. Stir in rice. Cook until golden brown, about 3 minutes, stirring often. Add to cooked vegetables. Makes 2 to 3 servings.

### Variations
**Pork, Chicken or Shrimp Fried Rice:** To make a main dish, omit bean sprouts, onion, green pepper and celery; add about 1/3 cup diced cooked pork, chicken or shrimp.

# Creamed Pea Combo

*A touch of dry sherry gives this vegetable trio a delicate flavor.*

1 (8-1/2-oz.) can peas
1 (8-oz.) can small whole stewed onions
2 tablespoons butter or margarine
1 tablespoon all-purpose flour
1 (2-1/2-oz.) jar mushrooms, drained

3/4 cup milk
1 tablespoon chicken broth
1 tablespoon dry sherry
Salt and pepper to taste

Prepare unit for open grilling. Drain peas and onions; reserve 1/2 cup liquid. Add liquid to preheated grill. Stir in peas and onions. Cook until heated through, about 5 minutes. Drain. Place in a medium bowl and keep warm. Melt butter or margarine on grill. Stir in flour. Add mushrooms, milk, chicken broth and sherry. Cook and stir until thickened, about 4 minutes. Pour over peas and onions. Season to taste with salt and pepper. Makes 3 to 4 servings.

---

*To make radish roses, cut the top off radishes and make 4 deep cuts along the edges. Cut a deep X in the center. Place in cold water in the refrigerator to open.*

# Cheese & Carrot Cakes

*The crunchy cashew coating makes these carrot-cheese-rice cakes irresistible.*

1 cup hot cooked rice
1/2 cup grated carrot
1/2 cup shredded process American cheese
1 egg, beaten

1 cup finely chopped salted cashews
1 teaspoon dried parsley flakes
1 tablespoon butter or margarine

Prepare unit for open grilling. In a small bowl, place rice, carrot, cheese and egg. Mix well. Form into 2 patties. In a shallow bowl, mix cashews and parsley. Coat patties with cashew mixture. On preheated grill, melt butter or margarine. Place patties in butter or margarine on grill. Cook until brown, about 1-1/2 minutes on each side. Makes 2 servings.

# Fresh Vegetable Stew

*You can use any type of summer squash or eggplant.*

2 tablespoons vegetable oil
1 zucchini, cut in 1/4-inch slices
1/4 cup chopped green pepper
1/4 cup chopped onion

1 garlic clove, minced
1 (8-oz.) can whole tomatoes
2 tablespoons snipped fresh parsley
Dash bottled hot pepper sauce

Prepare unit for open grilling. Add oil to preheated grill. Place zucchini, green pepper, onion and garlic on grill. Cook and stir until tender, about 5 minutes. Add tomatoes, parsley and hot pepper sauce. Cook and stir until heated through and tender, about 5 minutes. Makes 3 servings.

# Zucchini Patties

*Grated, unpeeled zucchini provides a nice, moist texture.*

2-1/2 tablespoons packaged biscuit mix
2 tablespoons grated Parmesan cheese
1/8 teaspoon salt
1/8 teaspoon garlic salt

1 egg, slightly beaten
1 cup finely grated unpeeled zucchini
  (1 medium)
Vegetable oil

Prepare unit for open grilling. In a medium bowl, mix biscuit mix, cheese, salt and garlic salt. Stir in beaten egg until mixture is just moistened. Fold in zucchini. Brush preheated grill with oil. Use about 1 tablespoon mixture for each patty. Cook until brown, about 1 minute on each side. Repeat, using remaining zucchini mixture. Makes 10 patties.

# *Grilled Breads*

Melt a little butter on your mini-grill, add a dash of flavored salt, some herbs or a little garlic, then put on thick slices of French bread to toast. French bread is delicious with any meal or on your break with coffee or tea.

Refrigerated rolls or biscuits, rolled on a floured surface to make a thin slice or bread stick, can be toasted in the herb butter. Sprinkle with sesame or poppy seeds for a pretty garnish.

Frozen waffles grill nicely. Keep them handy in your freezer for a fast breakfast. You can heat syrup or a honey and spice topping on your grill in about a minute.

Wake up to the heavenly aroma of homemade French toast. You'll enjoy the convenience of Overnight French Toast and the luxury of Strawberry French Toast.

If you're not a breakfast eater, give Mama's Chocolate Toast a chance. It's a tasty and easy beginning to a busy day.

# Toasted Cheese Slices

*Cheese spread stores well in refrigerator for handy use.*

1/2 (5-oz.) jar sharp process cheese spread with bacon
4 tablespoons butter or margarine, softened
1/2 teaspoon dry mustard

3 tablespoons butter or margarine, softened
9 French bread slices
Poppy seed or toasted sesame seed

In a small bowl, place cheese spread, 4 tablespoons butter or margarine and dry mustard. Beat with electric mixer on high speed until fluffy. Prepare unit for open grilling. On preheated grill, melt 1 tablespoon of remaining 3 tablespoons butter or margarine. Place 3 bread slices on grill. Cook until brown, about 1-1/2 minutes. Turn bread slices. Spread with cheese mixture and sprinkle with poppy or sesame seed. Cook until other side is brown, about another 1-1/2 minutes. Repeat with remaining butter, bread slices, cheese mixture and poppy or sesame seed. Makes 9 slices.

# Bacon Rolls

*A welcome change for breakfast.*

8 slices bacon
4 hot dog rolls

1 (5-oz.) jar pasteurized Neufchatel cheese spread with olive and pimiento

Prepare unit for open grilling. On preheated grill, partially cook bacon, 4 slices at a time, being careful to keep it limp and not crisp, 2-1/2 to 3 minutes. Drain drippings from grill. Halve hot dog rolls lengthwise to make 8 narrow rolls. Spread bottom of each narrow roll with cheese spread. Cover with tops. Wrap 1 slice bacon around each roll, securing with wooden picks. Prepare unit for closed grilling. Place rolls, 4 at a time, on grill. Close lid, but do not latch. Cook until bacon is done and roll is heated through, about 1-1/2 minutes. Makes 8 bacon rolls.

**Toasted Cheese Slices**

# Cheese-Herb Bread

*Grilled French bread sprinkled with herb-flavored cheese.*

3 tablespoons butter or margarine
2 slices French bread, cut 1-inch thick
2 tablespoons grated Parmesan cheese

1/4 teaspoon dried rosemary
1/4 teaspoon dried thyme

Prepare unit for open grilling. On preheated grill, melt butter or margarine. Place bread slices on grill and cook until brown, about 3 minutes. In a small bowl or cup, mix Parmesan cheese, rosemary and thyme. Turn bread slices and sprinkle with cheese-herb mixture. Cook until other side is brown, about 2 minutes. Makes 2 servings.

# Creamy Garlic Bread

*Creamy topping sets this garlic bread apart!*

1 (3-oz.) pkg. cream cheese, softened
2 tablespoons butter or margarine, softened
1/4 teaspoon garlic powder

3 tablespoons butter or margarine
2 slices French bread, cut 1-inch thick

Prepare unit for open grilling. In a small bowl, place cream cheese, 2 tablespoons butter or margarine and garlic powder; beat with electric mixer on high speed until smooth. On preheated grill, melt 3 tablespoons butter or margarine. Place bread slices on grill. Cook until brown, about 3 minutes. Turn; spread each slice with about 2 tablespoons creamy garlic mixture. Cook until other side is brown, about 2 minutes. Store remaining creamy garlic mixture in refrigerator for later use. Makes 2 servings.

# Garlic Bread Sticks

*Try these with Wilted Spinach Salad, page 115.*

1 (3.75-oz.) tube refrigerated biscuits
   (6 biscuits)
2 tablespoons sesame or poppy seed

2 tablespoons butter or margarine
1/2 teaspoon garlic salt

Prepare unit for open grilling. On a lightly floured surface, roll each biscuit into a thin pencil shape. Place sesame or poppy seed in a long shallow dish. Roll bread sticks in sesame or poppy seed. On preheated grill, melt butter or margarine. Stir in garlic salt. Place bread sticks on grill. Cook until brown and crisp, about 3 minutes, turning often. Makes 6 bread sticks.

# Herb-Seasoned Croutons

*Great for soups or salads—or just for munching!*

2 slices white bread
6 tablespoons butter or margarine

1 tablespoon dehydrated minced onion flakes
1 teaspoon dried marjoram

Prepare unit for closed grilling. Place bread slices on preheated grill. Close lid and latch handle. Cook until brown, about 3-1/2 minutes on each side. Remove and cut in 1/2-inch cubes. Prepare unit for open grilling. On preheated grill, melt butter or margarine. Stir in onion flakes and marjoram. Add bread cubes. Cook and stir until toasted, about 3 minutes. Makes 3/4 cup.

# Cinnamon-Honey Waffles

*You'll like this delicious syrup on pancakes and French toast, too!*

2 tablespoons vegetable oil
4 frozen waffles, thawed
1/2 cup honey

4 tablespoons butter or margarine, softened
1/4 cup raisins
1 teaspoon ground cinnamon

Prepare unit for open grilling. Add oil to preheated grill. Cook 2 waffles at a time until brown, about 2 minutes. Turn and cook until other side is brown, about 1-1/2 minutes. Remove and keep warm. Repeat with remaining 2 waffles. On preheated grill, combine honey, butter or margarine, raisins and cinnamon. Cook and stir until butter or margarine melts and syrup is heated, about 1-1/2 minutes. Serve over waffles. Makes 2 servings.

*Bread can be toasted on the grill with or without butter. Bread toasted without butter will usually take about twice as long to brown as buttered bread.*

# Strawberry French Toast

*Your brunch guests will return every weekend for this delicacy!*

2 slices bread, cut 1-inch thick
3 tablespoons strawberry preserves
1 tablespoon chopped pecans
1 egg, slightly beaten
1/3 cup milk

1-1/2 teaspoons sugar
1/4 teaspoon vanilla extract
2 tablespoons butter or margarine
2 tablespoons powdered sugar
1/4 cup fresh strawberries

Prepare unit for open grilling. Cut pocket in 1 side of each bread slice, cutting to other side, but not through. In a small bowl or cup, mix strawberry preserves and pecans. Stuff half the mixture into the pocket in each bread slice. In a pie plate, mix egg, milk, sugar and vanilla. On preheated grill, melt butter or margarine. Dip bread slices into egg mixture. Place on buttered grill. Cook until brown, about 2-1/2 minutes. Turn, sprinkle with half the powdered sugar. Cook until other side is brown, about another 2-1/2 minutes. Turn and sprinkle with remaining powdered sugar. Top with strawberries. Makes 2 servings.

## How to Make Strawberry French Toast

1/Cut a pocket in each thick bread slice, then spoon in a mixture of strawberry preserves and chopped nuts.

2/Dip the bread in egg batter. Cook until golden brown and top with powdered sugar and fresh strawberries.

# Overnight French Toast

*You'll never go back to your old method after you try this one!*

4 slices French bread, cut 1/2-inch thick
3 eggs
3/4 cup milk
1 tablespoon sugar

1/2 teaspoon vanilla extract
1/8 teaspoon salt
1 tablespoon butter or margarine
Powdered sugar or maple syrup

Arrange bread slices in a single layer in an 11" x 7" baking dish. In a small bowl, beat eggs, milk, sugar, vanilla and salt. Pour over bread slices. Turn bread slices to coat evenly. Cover and refrigerate several hours or overnight. Prepare unit for open grilling. On preheated grill, melt butter or margarine. Cook bread slices until golden brown, about 2 minutes on each side. Sprinkle with powdered sugar or serve with maple syrup. Makes 4 servings.

# Mama's Chocolate Toast

*A delicious variation of cinnamon toast!*

3 tablespoons sugar
1 teaspoon cocoa powder

Butter or margarine, softened
2 slices bread

Prepare unit for open grilling. In a small bowl or cup, mix sugar and cocoa. Spread butter or margarine on both sides of bread slices. Sprinkle both sides with cocoa-sugar mixture, shaking off excess. Cook on preheated grill until brown, about 1-1/2 minutes. Turn, sprinkle each slice again with about 1/2 teaspoon cocoa-sugar mixture and cook until brown, about 1-1/2 minutes. Remove from grill. Sprinkle other side of each slice with about 1/2 teaspoon of cocoa-sugar mixture. Makes 2 servings.

*Toaster pastries are quick and easy to heat on the mini-grill. On preheated open grill, melt about 2 tablespoons butter or margarine. Add pastries 2 at a time. Cook about 45 seconds to 1 minute on each side.*

# Desserts

Elegant desserts don't have to be time-consuming creations. Nor do they have to be heavily laden with thick pastry and rich toppings. Here are some desserts remarkable in their simplicity and irresistible in appearance and taste.

Many of the sweets in this section use fresh or canned fruit. Apple Brown Betty and Cranberry Crunch Parfaits are easy to make, fun to eat and not as soft on your waistline as a heavy gooey pastry. When a recipe calls for a topping of ice cream or whipped cream, be sensible; you need only a teaspoon to enjoy the flavor and texture.

Some occasions call for an extra-special effort and a super-rich treat. These recipes used with your mini-grill keep the effort down to a minimum and let you serve a treat worthy of an accomplished chef. Try Tropic Isle Banana Splits, Praline Sundaes or Chocolate-Mint Ice Cream Bars. Your guests will love them and, unless you tell them, they'll never guess how easy it all was!

# *Fruit Kabobs au Natural*

*Get out your skewers for this quick summertime treat.*

1 small peach, cut in 1-inch cubes
1 small apple, cut in 1-inch cubes
1 small banana, cut in 1-inch sections
3/4 cup fresh pineapple, cut in 1-inch cubes

3/4 cup fresh strawberries
1/4 cup honey
1 tablespoon lemon juice
4 tablespoons butter or margarine

Prepare unit for open grilling. Thread fruits alternately on 6 skewers. In a small bowl or cup, mix honey and lemon juice. On preheated grill, melt 2 tablespoons butter or margarine. Place 3 kabobs on grill. Cook until heated through, about 5 minutes, turning and brushing often with half of honey mixture. Repeat with remaining butter or margarine, kabobs and honey mixture. Makes about 6 kabobs.

# *Apple Brown Betty*

*A taste of good old-fashioned cooking.*

1 (3.75-oz.) tube refrigerated biscuits (6 biscuits)
1/2 cup brown sugar, firmly packed
1 tablespoon ground cinnamon
6 tablespoons butter or margarine
2 medium apples, pared, cored and cut in
   thin slices

1 tablespoon cornstarch
1 tablespoon brown sugar
1/2 teaspoon ground cinnamon
1 cup apple juice
1 teaspoon lemon juice
Ice cream or whipped topping

Prepare unit for open grilling. On a lightly floured surface, roll biscuits into 4-inch circles. In a pie plate, mix 1/2 cup brown sugar and 1 tablespoon cinnamon. Coat both sides of biscuits with sugar-cinnamon mixture. On preheated grill, melt 1 tablespoon butter or margarine. Add biscuits, 2 at a time, and cook until brown, 1/2 to 1 minute on each side. Remove and keep warm. Repeat with remaining biscuits and 2 tablespoons butter or margarine. Scrape excess sugar from grill. Melt remaining 3 tablespoons butter or margarine on grill. Add apple slices. Cook and stir until tender, about 8 minutes. Remove and keep warm. In a small bowl, mix cornstarch, 1 tablespoon brown sugar and 1/2 teaspoon cinnamon. Stir in apple juice. Pour onto grill. Cook and stir until thickened, about 2 minutes. Add lemon juice. Stir into apple slices. Layer in 3 dessert bowls: apple mixture, grilled biscuit and ice cream or whipped topping. Serve with additional grilled cinnamon biscuit. Makes 3 servings.

# Cranberry Crunch Parfaits

*The perfect dessert to follow a meal of leftover turkey.*

2 tablespoons butter or margarine
1/4 cup quick-cooking oats
2 tablespoons brown sugar
2 tablespoons chopped pecans
1/4 teaspoon ground cinnamon

1/2 cup water
1/2 cup granulated sugar
1 cup fresh cranberries
Vanilla ice cream

Prepare unit for open grilling. On preheated grill, melt butter or margarine. Add oats, brown sugar, pecans and cinnamon. Cook and stir until brown and crumbly, about 1 minute. Remove crumb toping and set aside. Pour water onto grill. Add granulated sugar; stir until dissolved. Add cranberries and cook until most skins pop, about 4 minutes. Layer in parfait glasses: ice cream, cranberries and crumb topping. Makes 2 to 3 servings.

## How to Make Cranberry Crunch Parfaits

**1/**Brown the oatmeal and pecan topping on the grill. Cook the cranberries and sugar in water until the skins pop.

**2/**Layer the ice cream, cranberries and crunch topping in parfait glasses or water goblets, then repeat the layers.

# Berry Peach Crisp

*Blueberries and peaches blend in an eye-catching dessert.*

4 tablespoons butter or margarine
1 cup quick-cooking oats
1/4 cup brown sugar, firmly packed
1 cup blueberry pie filling

1 (8-3/4-oz.) can peach slices, drained
1 tablespoon lemon juice
Whipped topping

Prepare unit for open grilling. On preheated grill, melt butter or margarine. Cook and stir oats and brown sugar until heated through, about 1-1/2 minutes. Divide mixture among 4 dessert bowls, reserving 1/4 cup for topping. Clean grill. Combine blueberry pie filling, peach slices and lemon juice on cold grill. Plug in grill. Cook and stir until filling and peach slices are heated through, about 4 minutes. Spoon over oat mixture. Top with whipped topping and reserved oat mixture. Makes 4 servings.

# Peach Melba Pudding

*Impress your guests with an elegant dessert!*

1 (10-oz.) pkg. frozen sweetened raspberries, thawed
2 tablespoons cornstarch

1 tablespoon Cherry Heering liqueur
2 canned or fresh peach halves
2 (5-oz.) cans vanilla pudding

Prepare unit for open grilling. Drain raspberries; reserve syrup. On cold grill, combine cornstarch and syrup. Plug in grill. Cook and stir syrup until thickened and clear, about 4 minutes. Stir in raspberries and Cherry Heering liqueur. Cook and stir until heated through, about 1 minute. Cool. Layer in 2 sherbet glasses: peach halves, some raspberry sauce, pudding and more raspberry sauce. Makes 2 servings.

# Praline Sundaes

*The smooth butterscotch-pecan sauce is too good to resist.*

1 egg yolk, slightly beaten
1/3 cup brown sugar, firmly packed
3 tablespoons light corn syrup
2 tablespoons chopped pecans

2 tablespoons water
2 tablespoons butter or margarine
Vanilla ice cream

Prepare unit for open grilling. On cold grill, combine all ingredients except ice cream. Plug in grill. Cook and stir until mixture thickens and boils, about 8 minutes. Serve over ice cream. Makes 1/2 cup sauce.

# Tropic Isle Banana Splits

*Try this flaming extravaganza at your next dinner party.*

4 tablespoons butter or margarine
1/4 cup shredded coconut
1/4 cup brown sugar, firmly packed
1/2 teaspoon ground cinnamon
1 cup fresh peach slices or 1 (8-3/4-oz.)
   can peach slices, drained

1/4 cup heated rum
2 small bananas, split lengthwise
Vanilla, chocolate and strawberry ice cream
Maraschino cherries, if desired

Prepare unit for open grilling. On preheated grill, melt butter or margarine. Add coconut. Cook and stir until toasted, about 2 minutes. Remove coconut and set aside; reserve butter or margarine on grill. Stir in brown sugar and cinnamon. Add peaches. Cook and stir until heated through, about 3-1/2 minutes. Unplug grill. Ignite heated rum and pour over peaches. Cook and stir peaches until flame subsides. Line 2 banana split dishes with banana halves. Top with scoops of vanilla, chocolate and strawberry ice cream. Drizzle with cooked peaches. Sprinkle with toasted coconut. Top with maraschino cherries, if desired. Makes 2 servings.

# Chocolate-Mint Ice Cream Bars

*Use your favorite ice cream to vary the flavor of this crunchy bar.*

4 tablespoons butter or margarine
2 cups crushed cream-filled chocolate cookies
   (about 16)
1 qt. mint chocolate chip ice cream, softened

4 tablespoons butter or margarine
1/2 cup flaked coconut
1/2 cup chopped pecans

Prepare unit for open grilling. On preheated grill, melt 4 tablespoons butter or margarine. In a 9" x 5" baking dish, mix melted butter or margarine and 1-3/4 cups of the crumbs. Pat into bottom of dish to form a crust. Spread softened ice cream on crust and place in freezer. On preheated grill, melt remaining 4 tablespoons butter or margarine. Stir in coconut and pecans. Cook and stir until coconut is lightly toasted, about 2 minutes. Add remaining 1/4 cup cookie crumbs. Cool. Sprinkle cooled pecan mixture on top of ice cream. Freeze 2 hours or more. Remove from freezer 15 minutes before serving. Cut into squares. Makes 8 servings.

# Double Fudge Sundaes

*Put off making this until your figure can afford it.*

1 (5-1/3-oz.) can evaporated milk
1 (6-oz.) pkg. chocolate chips (1 cup)
1/2 (1-pt.) jar marshmallow creme
Chocolate ice cream

Whipped topping
Chopped nuts
Maraschino cherries, if desired

Prepare unit for open grilling. On cold grill, combine milk and chocolate chips. Plug in grill. Cook and stir until chocolate chips just melt, 1 to 2 minutes. Pour into a medium bowl. Stir in marshmallow creme. Beat until melted. Serve over chocolate ice cream. Spoon on whipped topping and nuts. Top with maraschino cherries, if desired. Makes about 1-3/4 cups sauce.

# Fluffy Coconut Torte

*Rich layers of cake and pudding with creamy coconut frosting.*

1 (3-3/4-oz.) pkg. coconut cream instant
    pudding mix
2 cups milk
1 (10-3/4-oz.) frozen pound cake, thawed
3 tablespoons all-purpose flour

1 cup milk
1/2 cup shortening
4 tablespoons butter or margarine, softened
1/2 cup sugar
Shredded coconut for garnish

Prepare instant pudding with 2 cups milk according to package directions. The brand of pudding mix I used called for 2 cups of milk per package. If you use another brand, the amount of milk may vary. Chill. Split pound cake lengthwise to form 3 layers. Spread chilled pudding on 2 of the layers and top with the third layer; chill. Prepare unit for open grilling. Combine flour and 1/4 cup of the 1 cup milk to form a paste. Stir in remaining milk; cook and stir on preheated grill until thickened, about 1-1/2 to 2 minutes. Chill. Cream shortening and butter with electric mixer on medium speed in mixing bowl. Gradually beat in sugar. When sauce is chilled, add to shortening mixture; beat until fluffy. Frost cake with frosting and sprinkle with coconut. Makes 8 servings.

---

*Two tablespoons flour or 1 tablespoon cornstarch is the standard for thickening 1 cup liquid.*
*If you desire a thicker or thinner consistency, adjust thickening agent or liquid accordingly.*

# Summertime Strawberry Tarts

*Enjoy these tarts all year 'round—use frozen strawberries for Wintertime Strawberry Tarts.*

1-1/4 cups fresh or thawed frozen
  strawberries
2 dessert shells
1/4 cup water

2 tablespoons sugar
2 teaspoons cornstarch
Whipped topping

Prepare unit for open grilling. Halve strawberries. Place 1/2 cup of the strawberries in each dessert shell. Crush remaining 1/4 cup strawberries; add water. Cook on preheated grill until softened, about 1 minute. Press through a sieve. In a small bowl, mix sugar and cornstarch; gradually stir sieved strawberry juice into sugar-cornstarch mixture. Pour onto grill. Cook and stir until thickened and clear, about 2-1/2 minutes. Pour over halved strawberries in dessert shells. Refrigerate. Top with whipped topping before serving. Makes 2 servings.

# Sunny Lemon Tarts

*Pucker up!*

3/4 cup sugar
3 tablespoons cornstarch
1 cup hot water
2 egg yolks
1 tablespoon butter or margarine

1 teaspoon grated lemon peel
1/4 cup lemon juice
4 dessert shells
Whipped topping

Prepare unit for open grilling. On cold grill, combine sugar and cornstarch. Plug in grill. Gradually stir in hot water. Cook and stir until thickened and clear, about 3 minutes. Unplug grill. Spoon a small amount, about 1/4 cup, of sugar-cornstarch mixture into egg yolks; mix well. Return to cornstarch mixture on grill. Add butter or margarine and lemon peel. Stir until butter or margarine is melted. Pour into medium bowl. Add lemon juice. Beat well until smooth. Spoon into dessert shells. Top with whipped topping. Makes 4 tarts.

# Chocolate-Pistachio Pie

*Favorite flavors for an elegant gathering to enjoy.*

2 (3-3/4-oz.) pkgs. pistachio instant
   pudding mix
4 cups milk
1 (9-inch) graham cracker pie shell
1 (1-oz.) square unsweetened chocolate
2/3 cup sweetened condensed milk

1/8 teaspoon salt
1/4 teaspoon vanilla extract
1/2 cup whipped topping
Whipped topping, shaved chocolate or
   chopped pistachios for garnish

Prepare instant pudding with milk according to package directions. The brand of pudding mix I used called for 2 cups of milk per package. If you use another brand, the amount of milk may vary. Spread half the pudding into pie shell; refrigerate. Refrigerate remaining pudding for later use. Prepare unit for open grilling. Chop chocolate square into small pieces. On cold grill, combine chocolate pieces, sweetened condensed milk and salt. Plug in grill. Cook and stir until chocolate melts and mixture begins to thicken, about 6 minutes. Remove from heat. Stir in vanilla extract. Chill mixture until cool. Fold 1/2 cup whipped topping into cooled chocolate mixture. Pour over pudding in pie shell; spread evenly. Top with remaining pudding, spreading evenly. Refrigerate about 4 hours before serving. Garnish with additional whipped topping, shaved chocolate or chopped pistachios. Makes one 9-inch pie.

# Blueberry & Cream Cheese Pie

*This blue ribbon dessert will enhance any meal!*

1 (8-oz.) pkg. cream cheese, softened
1 (14-oz.) can sweetened condensed milk
1/2 cup lemon juice
1 teaspoon vanilla extract
1 (9-inch) graham cracker pie shell

3/4 cup sugar
2 tablespoons cornstarch
2 cups fresh or thawed frozen blueberries
1/2 cup water

In a medium bowl, beat softened cream cheese with electric mixer on high speed until light and fluffy. With mixer on medium speed, gradually stir in sweetened condensed milk. Beat until thoroughly blended. Stir in lemon juice and vanilla extract. Pour into pie shell. Refrigerate 2 to 3 hours. Prepare unit for open grilling. On cold grill, combine sugar and cornstarch. Crush 1/2 cup of the blueberries; reserve remaining blueberries. Add crushed blueberries and water to sugar mixture on grill. Plug in grill. Cook and stir until blueberry mixture is thickened and clear, about 3 minutes. Cool. Arrange remaining blueberries on top of pie. Pour cooled glaze over chilled pie. Chill before serving. Makes one 9-inch pie.

# Cinnamon-Apple Turnovers

*Crisp-fried turnovers are sure to disappear as soon as you take them off the grill.*

1 tablespoon all-purpose flour
1 tablespoon brown sugar
Dash ground cinnamon
Dash ground nutmeg
1/2 cup chopped pared apple
1 tablespoon raisins

1 stick pastry mix
2 tablespoons water
3 tablespoons vegetable oil
About 2 teaspoons granulated sugar
2 tablespoons granulated sugar
1/2 teaspoon ground cinnamon

In a medium bowl, mix flour, brown sugar, dash cinnamon and nutmeg. Toss with apple and raisins. Set apple filling aside. Prepare pastry with water according to package directions. Roll out dough to a 12-inch square. Cut into nine 4-inch squares. Spoon apple filling on half of each square. Fold other half over filling to form a triangle. Moisten edges of pastry and seal with tines of a fork. Prepare unit for open grilling. Pour oil onto preheated grill. Cook turnovers, 3 at a time, until brown, about 3 minutes on each side. In a small bowl or cup, mix granulated sugar and cinnamon. Sprinkle over browned turnovers. Makes 9 turnovers.

## How to Make Cinnamon-Apple Turnovers

1/Spoon the raisin and apple filling onto a half of each pastry square.

2/Moisten the edges of the pastry with water, then fold over and seal with tines of a fork.

# Snacks & Appetizers

Plan your next party around the versatile mini-grill. Have some of the delicious appetizers in this section ready for your guests to cook on the grill. This lets them join in the cooking fun and it's easy on you. A good starter is Polynesian Dipped Chicken. And if you want to keep your recipe for Orange-Glazed Hors d'Oeuvres a secret, go ahead; they'll never be able to guess all the ingredients. Place bowls of nibbles from the grill around the room. Bowls of Chili-Cheese Dip with taco chips and platters of Three-Cheese Balls will keep the guests moving and the conversation going.

When the hungry crew comes in from school, work or shopping, have some cookies waiting. A plate of Chocolate Oatmeal Drops is a natural with big glasses of cold milk. Or how about a creamy dip with vegetable dippers? Crisp Eggplant Strips with Creamy Garlic Dip make a delicious and nutritious snack.

If you want to heat soup, pour a 1- or 2-cup serving—whatever your grill will hold—onto the mini-grill. It will heat in just a few minutes.

# Hot Crab Dip

*Watch your guests line up for this rich creamy dip.*

2 tablespoons butter or margarine
1/2 (6-oz.) pkg. frozen crabmeat, thawed
    and finely chopped
1 (3-oz.) pkg. cream cheese, cut in pieces
1/4 cup milk

1/4 cup shredded process American cheese
    (1-oz.)
2 tablespoons chopped pimiento
Dash garlic salt

Prepare unit for open grilling. On preheated grill, melt butter or margarine. Add crabmeat. Cook and stir until heated through, about 2 minutes. Remove and keep warm. Clean grill. On cold grill, combine cream cheese, milk, American cheese, pimiento and garlic salt. Plug in grill. Cook and stir until cheeses melt, about 4 minutes. Place in a medium bowl. Stir in crabmeat. Makes about 3/4 cup.

# Crisp Eggplant Sticks
# With Creamy Garlic Dip

*Try a store-bought dip instead of Creamy Garlic Dip for a quick substitute.*

1 medium eggplant,
    cut in 1/2" x 1/2" x 3" strips
Garlic salt to taste
1 cup all-purpose flour

1/2 teaspoon garlic salt
1/8 teaspoon pepper
1/4 cup vegetable oil
Creamy Garlic Dip, see below

*Creamy Garlic Dip:*
2 (3-oz.) pkgs. cream cheese, softened
1/3 cup milk

1/4 cup chopped green onion
1/2 teaspoon garlic powder

Prepare unit for open grilling. Sprinkle eggplant strips with garlic salt to taste. In a pie plate, mix flour, 1/2 teaspoon garlic salt and pepper. Roll eggplant strips in flour mixture to coat. Add oil to preheated grill. Cook eggplant strips, half at a time, until golden brown, about 5 minutes, turning often. Drain on paper towels. Serve with Creamy Garlic Dip. Makes about 20 sticks.

Creamy Garlic Dip:
In a small bowl, combine all ingredients. Beat with electric mixer on medium speed until smooth. Makes about 1 cup.

# Frank Kabobs Deluxe

*Tangy, glazed kabobs with a lot of style. Use your most elegant skewers.*

1 (6-oz.) jar marinated artichoke hearts or crowns
1 (2-1/2-oz.) pkg. smoked sliced beef

1 (5-oz.) pkg. smoky cocktail link sausage
12 cherry tomatoes
4 dill pickle spears, cut in thirds

Prepare unit for open grilling. Drain artichokes; reserve marinade. Wrap artichokes in sliced beef. Thread alternately on 6 skewers: artichokes, cocktail links, tomatoes and pickles. On preheated grill, place 3 kabobs. Cook until heated through, about 5 minutes, turning and brushing often with reserved marinade. Repeat with remaining kabobs. Makes 6 servings.

# Cheese-Chili Dip

*A great rarebit sauce for topping burgers and sandwiches.*

1 (8-oz.) jar taco sauce
1 tablespoon all-purpose flour
2 cups shredded process American cheese (8-oz.)

Corn chips
Vegetable dippers

Prepare unit for open grilling. In a small bowl, mix taco sauce and flour. Stir until smooth. On cold grill, combine taco sauce and flour mixture with cheese. Plug in grill. Cook and stir until cheese melts and mixture boils, 2 to 3 minutes. Serve with corn chips and vegetable dippers. Makes 1-1/2 cups.

**Frank Kabobs Deluxe**

# *Polynesian Dipped Chicken*

*Good enough to make a meal of!*

4 chicken wings
Seasoned coating mix for chicken
1/2 cup vegetable oil

1/4 cup pineapple preserves
1/2 teaspoon prepared mustard
1/2 teaspoon prepared horseradish

Prepare unit for open grilling. Prepare chicken wings according to directions for coating mix. Add oil to preheated grill. Cook chicken in oil until done, about 18 minutes, turning several times. In a small bowl, mix preserves, mustard and horseradish. Serve dip with chicken wings. Makes 4 chicken wings.

# *Three-Cheese Balls*

*Especially good during the holiday season!*

1 (3-oz.) pkg. cream cheese, softened
1 cup shredded Cheddar cheese (4 oz.)
1/2 cup crumbled blue cheese (2 oz.)

Chopped nuts
2 tablespoons butter or margarine

In a medium bowl, with electric mixer on high speed, beat cream cheese, Cheddar cheese and blue cheese until blended. Chill. Shape into 1-inch balls. Roll in nuts. Prepare unit for open grilling. On preheated grill, melt butter or margarine. Add cheese balls. Cook until toasted, about 2-1/2 minutes, turning often. Makes 10 balls.

---

*Accurate measuring is a must for recipe success. Use standard measuring equipment rather than kitchen spoons and cups. Bent or dented measuring equipment also results in inaccurate measures.*

# *Orange-Glazed Hors d'Oeuvres*

*Whip these up on a moment's notice!*

1 (8-oz.) can Vienna sausage
1/2 cup orange marmalade
1 tablespoon dry sherry

1 tablespoon lemon juice
1 tablespoon  Dijon-style mustard

Prepare unit for open grilling. On preheated grill, cook Vienna sausage until heated through, about 4 minutes, turning several times. In a small bowl, mix orange marmalade, sherry, lemon juice and mustard. Pour glaze over sausage. Cook until hot, about 3 minutes, turning sausage and spooning glaze over several times. Serve on wooden picks. Makes 2 to 4 servings.

# *Easy Nuts & Bolts*

*You'll enjoy TV more with a bowl of tasty-crunchy snacks.*

3 tablespoons butter or margarine
1 tablespoon salad seasoning
1 teaspoon Worcestershire sauce
1/2 teaspoon garlic salt

1 cup pretzel sticks
1/2 cup peanuts
1/2 cup small square corn, wheat or rice cereal

Prepare unit for open grilling. On preheated grill, melt butter or margarine. Stir in salad seasoning, Worcestershire sauce and garlic salt. Add pretzels, peanuts and cereal. Cook and toss until heated through and toasted, about 1-1/2 minutes. Makes about 2 cups.

# Parmesan Potato & Onion Crunch

*Try this as a quick party snack or a take-along to the drive-in theater.*

3 tablespoons butter or margarine
1 (13-oz.) can French-fried onions
1 (1.5-oz.) can shoestring potatoes

1/4 cup grated Parmesan cheese
2 teaspoons Italian salad dressing mix

Prepare unit for open grilling. On preheated grill, melt half the butter or margarine. Add onions, tossing to coat with butter or margarine. Cook and stir until heated through, about 1-1/2 minutes. Place in a medium bowl. Repeat with remaining butter or margarine and potatoes. Add potatoes to bowl with onions. Sprinkle with Parmesan cheese and salad dressing mix. Makes about 2 cups.

# Nutty Caramel Apples

*Bourbon subtly flavors an old favorite!*

1 tablespoon butter or margarine
3/4 cup caramel ice cream topping
1 tablespoon bourbon

2 apples, cored and cut in wedges
Chopped pecans

Prepare unit for open grilling. On preheated grill, melt butter or margarine. Stir in ice cream topping and bourbon. Cook and stir to blend well and heat through, about 1-1/2 minutes. Unplug grill. Dip and roll apples in caramel mixture and then in pecans. Makes 4 servings.

# Bob's Chicken Niblets

*Good finger food for your cocktail hour.*

1/2 cup all-purpose flour
3/4 teaspoon salt
1/2 teaspoon baking powder
1 egg, beaten
1/3 cup milk

2 tablespoons vegetable oil
1 uncooked chicken breast,
    boned and cut in 1-inch cubes
1/4 cup vegetable oil

Prepare unit for open grilling. In a medium bowl, stir together flour, salt and baking powder. In a small bowl, mix egg, milk and 2 tablespoons oil. Add to flour mixture. Stir until smooth. Dip chicken cubes in batter. Add 1/4 cup oil to preheated grill. Cook chicken cubes in hot oil until golden brown, about 7 minutes, turning several times. Makes 4 servings.

## How to Make Bob's Chicken Niblets

1/With a sharp knife, cut boned chicken breast into 1-inch cubes.

2/Dip the chicken cubes in batter. Fry in hot oil until golden brown.

# Sautéed Bananas

*Popular in Latin America. A friend from El Salvador likes his with sweetened dairy sour cream.*

**2 tablespoons butter or margarine**
**1 firm banana, split lengthwise**

**2 tablespoons brown sugar**

Prepare unit for open grilling. On preheated grill, melt butter or margarine. Place banana halves on grill. Sprinkle with brown sugar. Cook, brushing with melted butter or margarine, until bananas are heated through, turning occasionally, about 6 minutes. Cut in 1-inch pieces. Serve on wooden picks. Makes 2 servings.

# Easy Chocolate Fudge

*Fudge on your burger cooker? Why not!*

**2/3 cup sugar**
**1/4 cup evaporated milk**
**1 tablespoon butter or margarine**
**1/2 (6-oz.) pkg. chocolate chips (1/2 cup)**

**1/3 (4-oz.) bar German sweet chocolate**
  **(6 squares), chopped**
**1/2 cup chopped pecans**
**1/4 cup marshmallow creme**

Prepare unit for open grilling. Butter a 9" x 5" loaf dish. On cold grill, combine sugar, evaporated milk and butter or margarine. Plug in grill. Cook and stir until boiling, about 3 minutes. In a medium bowl, mix chocolate chips, German sweet chocolate, pecans and marshmallow creme. Pour boiling liquid from grill over chocolate mixture; stir well. Pour into buttered loaf dish. Cool. Cut into squares. Makes about 2/3 pound.

# Chocolate-Bourbon Balls

*These keep well—if you hide them!*

| | |
|---|---|
| 1 (6-oz.) pkg. chocolate chips (1 cup) | 1 cup chopped pecans |
| 1/3 cup bourbon | 1/2 cup sifted powdered sugar |
| 3 tablespoons light corn syrup | Granulated sugar |
| 2-1/2 cups vanilla wafer crumbs | |

Prepare unit for open grilling. On cold grill, combine chocolate chips, bourbon and corn syrup. Plug in grill. Cook and stir until chocolate chips begin to melt, about 1 minute. Place in a large bowl and stir until chips melt. Add wafer crumbs, pecans and powdered sugar. Mix well. Let stand about 30 minutes. Form into 1-inch balls. Roll in granulated sugar. Let season in covered container for several days. Makes about 36 balls.

# Chocolate Coconut Balls

*Anyone for rich chocolate candy?*

| | |
|---|---|
| 1 (6-oz.) pkg. chocolate chips (1 cup) | 1/3 cup chopped walnuts |
| 1/2 cup sweetened condensed milk | 1 teaspoon vanilla extract |
| 2 cups flaked coconut | |

Prepare unit for open grilling. On cold grill, combine chocolate chips and sweetened condensed milk. Plug in grill. Cook and stir until chocolate chips begin to melt and milk is heated through, about 2 minutes. Place in a large bowl and stir until chips melt. Stir in coconut, walnuts and vanilla extract. Chill for 15 minutes. Roll into 1-inch balls. Makes about 24 balls.

# Coconut-Mallow Squares

*A great make-it-yourself after school snack!*

1 (3-1/8-oz.) pkg. regular coconut cream
   pudding mix
1/2 cup light corn syrup

1/2 (1-pt.) jar marshmallow creme
4 cups crisp rice cereal

Prepare unit for open grilling. Butter an 8-inch square baking dish. On cold grill, combine pudding mix and corn syrup. Plug in grill. Cook and stir to blend well until mixture is bubbly, about 3 minutes. Place marshmallow creme in a large bowl. Add hot syrup. Beat with wooden spoon until blended. Fold in rice cereal. Turn into buttered baking dish. Cool and cut into bars. Makes about 16 bars.

## How to Make Coconut-Mallow Squares

**1/On the cold grill, combine coconut pudding mix and corn syrup. Plug in grill and stir until mixture is bubbly.**

**2/Beat the hot pudding mixture into the marshmallow creme, then fold in crisp rice cereal.**

# Chocolate-Oatmeal Drops

*A moist cookie that's sure to please everyone.*

| | |
|---|---|
| 1-1/2 cups quick-cooking oats | 1/3 cup milk |
| 1/4 cup flaked coconut | 4 tablespoons butter or margarine, softened |
| 3 tablespoons cocoa powder | 1/4 cup chopped pecans |
| 1 cup sugar | 1 teaspoon vanilla extract |

Prepare unit for open grilling. In a large bowl, mix oats, coconut and cocoa; set aside. On cold grill, combine sugar, milk and butter or margarine. Plug in grill. Cook and stir until boiling, about 2-1/2 minutes. Continue cooking for 1/2 minute, stirring often. Pour sugar mixture over oat mixture. Add pecans and vanilla extract. Mix well. Drop by teaspoonfuls on waxed paper. The mixture will be moist. Let set about an hour before serving. Makes about 24 cookies.

# Peanut Butter & Fudge Sandwiches

*Peanut butter and chocolate—how can you miss?*

| | |
|---|---|
| 1 (6-oz.) pkg. peanut butter chips (1 cup) | 1 (6-oz.) pkg. chocolate chips (1 cup) |
| 1/2 cup light corn syrup | 1/2 cup sifted powdered sugar |
| 2 tablespoons butter or margarine, softened | 2 tablespoons butter or margarine, softened |
| 4 cups crisp rice cereal | 1 tablespoon water |

Prepare unit for open grilling. Butter an 8-inch square baking dish. On cold grill, combine peanut butter chips, corn syrup and 2 tablespoons butter or margarine. Plug in grill. Cook and stir until chips begin to melt, about 2 minutes. Place in a large bowl and stir mixture until chips melt. Add cereal. Stir to coat well with peanut butter mixture. Press half the cereal mixture into buttered baking dish. Chill. Set remaining cereal mixture aside. Clean grill. On cold grill, combine chocolate chips, powdered sugar, 2 tablespoons butter or margarine and water. Plug in grill. Cook and stir until chips begin to melt, about 1 minute. Remove from heat and stir until chips melt. Spread over chilled mixture. Spread remaining cereal mixture evenly over top. Press gently. Chill about 1 hour or until firm. Cut into 1-1/2-inch squares. Makes about 24 squares.

# Toasted Coconut Macaroons

*Especially for coconut lovers*

3 tablespoons butter or margarine

2 cups flaked coconut

1/2 cup granola

1/2 cup sweetened condensed milk

1 teaspoon almond extract

Prepare unit for open grilling. On preheated grill, melt butter or margarine. Add coconut. Cook and stir until golden brown, about 5 minutes. In a large bowl, mix granola and sweetened condensed milk. Stir in toasted coconut and almond extract. Chill for 15 minutes. Roll into 1-inch balls. Makes about 18 cookies.

# Lemon Ice Balls

*Very delicately flavored.*

4 tablespoons butter or margarine

1/2 cup frozen lemonade concentrate, thawed

1 (7-1/4-oz.) box vanilla wafers, crushed

1 cup powdered sugar

Powdered sugar

Prepare unit for open grilling. On preheated grill, melt butter or margarine. Add lemonade concentrate. Cook and stir until heated through, about 2 minutes. In a large bowl, mix vanilla wafers and 1 cup powdered sugar. Add lemonade concentrate mixture to vanilla wafer mixture. Shape into 1-inch balls. Roll in powdered sugar. Makes about 24 balls.

# Menus

You can count on your mini-grill to turn out an entire dinner—even if you're in a situation where it's your only means of cooking. Here are some sample menus to get started on.

If you're single and want to impress someone important in your life with a gourmet dinner, Candlelight Dinner for Two with Steak Diane Flambé and Cherries Jubilee will set the right mood for the evening. Don't forget to buy candles!

There's no place like home, even if it is a dormitory room. With a mini-grill on hand, you can cook Chili-Cheese Hamburgers and Crunchy S'Mores for your roommate or best friend.

A houseful of teenagers? Get out your mini-grill and let them cook their own Miniature Sausage Pizzas with Peanutty Popcorn Balls for dessert.

Maybe you like to cook, but not when you have to eat alone. Then the Solo Meal with a Gourmet Touch is for you. It includes Rice-Stuffed Trout and Devilishly Good Corn on the Cob. Perhaps there are just the two of you and the cooking-eating routine is getting a little humdrum. Quick & Easy Dinner for Two shows you how to make both a delicious stew and Cheese-Corn Cakes on your mini-grill.

If you're traveling across country or on a weekend camping trip in your motor home, the mini-grill is the perfect appliance. Try the Hearty Campers' Breakfast with Farmers' Scramble and Grilled Honey Buns or Super Cinnamon Toast.

**After you've grilled corn in mustard-butter you'll never eat it plain again!**

## How to Make
## Devilishly Good Corn on the Cob

## Devilishly Good Corn on the Cob

*Try deviled corn for a change—you'll like it!*

| | |
|---|---|
| 1 tablespoon butter or margarine | 1/4 teaspoon celery salt |
| 1/2 teaspoon prepared mustard | 1 ear corn on the cob |

Prepare unit for open grilling. On preheated grill, melt butter or margarine. Stir in mustard and celery salt. Add corn. Cook until done, about 3 minutes, turning often. Makes 1 serving.

1/Spoon the lemon-rice filling into a fresh or thawed frozen trout.

2/Wind strips of bacon around the trout to add flavor and hold the stuffing.

*How to Make Rice-Stuffed Trout*

# Rice-Stuffed Trout

*Pamper yourself with this delicately flavored trout.*

| | |
|---|---|
| 1 tablespoon butter or margarine | 2 teaspoons lemon juice |
| 1 tablespoon chopped celery | 1/4 teaspoon grated lemon peel |
| 1 tablespoon chopped onion | 1 (8-oz.) trout, pan-dressed |
| 1/4 cup cooked rice | 2 slices bacon |
| 1 tablespoon chopped pimiento | |

Prepare unit for open grilling. On preheated grill, melt butter or margarine. Add celery and onion. Cook and stir until tender, about 2 minutes. Combine celery mixture, cooked rice, pimiento, lemon juice and lemon peel. Toss well. Stuff trout with rice mixture. Wind bacon around trout and secure with wooden picks. Prepare unit for closed grilling. Place fish on grill. Close lid, but do not latch. Cook until bacon is brown and fish flakes easily with a fork, about 5-1/2 minutes on each side. Makes 1 serving.

Cheese is the built-in garnish for this deluxe juicy burger with dressed-up canned chili.

## How to Make Chili-Cheese Hamburgers

# Chili-Cheese Hamburgers

*Treat yourself to paper plates to make a no-work meal.*

| | |
|---|---|
| 1 tablespoon butter or margarine | 1 teaspoon dehydrated minced onion flakes |
| 2 hamburger rolls, split | 1 teaspoon prepared mustard |
| 8 oz. ground beef or bulk pork sausage | 1 teaspoon Worcestershire sauce |
| 1 (7-1/2-oz.) can hot chili with beans | 1/4 cup shredded American cheese (1-oz.) |

Prepare unit for open grilling. On preheated grill, melt butter or margarine. Toast rolls, cut side down, until brown, 1 to 1-1/2 minutes. Remove and keep warm. Shape meat into 2 patties. Cook until brown, 2-1/2 to 3 minutes on each side for rare. Place on top of toasted rolls and keep warm. Combine chili, onion flakes, mustard and Worcestershire sauce on grill. Cook and stir until heated through, about 1-1/2 minutes. Spoon over hamburgers on toasted rolls. Top with cheese and roll halves. Makes 2 burgers.

1/Spread half the graham cracker squares with marshmallow creme and top the remaining crackers with miniature chocolate bars.

2/In just 1-1/2 minutes the chocolate will be melted and gooey—ready to be sandwiched with the marshmallow half for S'Mores!

## How to Make Crunchy S'Mores

## Crunchy S'Mores

*Chocolate crackle bars add a crunch to your old favorites.*

2 (1-1/8-oz.) chocolate crackle bars *or*      8 squares graham crackers
   8 miniature bars                       4 tablespoons marshmallow creme

Prepare unit for open grilling. Place chocolate bars on half the graham crackers. Spread remaining graham crackers with marshmallow creme. Place 2 graham crackers with chocolate bars and 2 graham crackers with marshmallow creme open-face on preheated grill. Cook until chocolate begins to melt and marshmallow creme is heated, about 1-1/2 minutes. Press chocolate and marshmallow creme halves together. Repeat with remaining chocolate and marshmallow creme halves. Makes 4 S'Mores.

## Teenager's Pizza Party

### Menu
Miniature Sausage Pizzas
Vegetable Dippers
Sour Cream Dip
Soft Drinks
Peanutty Popcorn Balls
Crisp Apples

With buttered hands, shape the peanut-butter-coated popcorn and peanuts into balls—let everyone join in the fun.

## How to Make
## Peanutty Popcorn Balls

# Peanutty Popcorn Balls

*Just enough peanuts and popcorn to round out a satisfying meal.*

3 cups popped popcorn
1/2 cup salted peanuts
1/2 cup brown sugar, firmly packed

1/2 cup light corn syrup
1/4 cup peanut butter
1 teaspoon vanilla extract

Prepare unit for open grilling. In a large bowl, mix popcorn and peanuts; set aside. On preheated grill, combine sugar and corn syrup. Cook and stir until brown sugar dissolves and mixture boils, about 3 minutes. Place peanut butter and vanilla in a small bowl. Quickly stir in hot syrup mixture. Pour over popcorn mixture at once. Stir to coat well. With buttered hands, form into balls. Makes 6 popcorn balls.

1/While you're browning the sausage and spices on the grill, roll refrigerated biscuits on a floured surface, enlarging them to 4-inch circles.

2/Top the biscuit rounds with tomato paste, garlic salt, oregano, sausage and mozzarella. Grill for 2 minutes.

## How to Make Miniature Sausage Pizzas

# Miniature Sausage Pizzas

*Mini-pizzas teens enjoy fixing—not to mention eating!*

8 oz. bulk pork sausage
1 garlic clove, minced
1/2 teaspoon ground cumin
1 (3.75-oz.) tube refrigerated biscuits
  (6 biscuits)

2 tablespoons tomato paste
Dried oregano to taste
Dash garlic salt
1 cup shredded mozzarella cheese (4 oz.)
1 tablespoon vegetable oil

Prepare unit for open grilling. Crumble sausage onto preheated grill. Add garlic and cumin. Cook and stir until brown, about 4 minutes. Remove sausage. Drain grill. On lightly floured surface, roll each biscuit to a circle 4 inches in diameter. Spread each biscuit with 1 teaspoon of the tomato paste. Sprinkle with oregano and garlic salt. Top with sausage and cheese. Add oil to preheated grill. Cook pizzas 2 at a time until crusts are brown, about 2 minutes. Makes 6 mini-pizzas.

Spread honey buns with butter or margarine. Toast on grill until golden brown.

*How to Make
Grilled Honey Buns*

# Grilled Honey Buns

*Be sure to take plenty along—they'll ask for seconds.*

3 tablespoons butter or margarine,
  softened

2 honey buns
Chopped nuts

Prepare unit for open grilling. Spread 1/2 tablespoon of the butter or margarine on 1 side of each honey bun. On preheated grill, melt remaining butter or margarine. Place honey buns on grill buttered side up. Cook until toasted, about 1-1/2 minutes on each side. Top with nuts. Makes 2 servings.

# Super Cinnamon Toast

*Start your day with a little spice. It goes so well with coffee!*

2 tablespoons butter or margarine, softened
2 slices raisin bread

2 tablespoons brown sugar
1/2 teaspoon ground cinnamon

Prepare unit for closed grilling. Butter bread generously on both sides. Place on preheated grill. Close cover, but do not latch. Cook until toasted, about 4 minutes on each side. In a small bowl or cup, mix brown sugar and cinnamon. Coat toast generously with cinnamon-sugar mixture. Makes 2 slices.

1/Slice green onions, dice ham and canned potatoes before mixing with eggs.

2/Top the scrambled egg and ham mixture with shredded Cheddar cheese.

## How to Make Farmers' Scramble

# Farmers' Scramble

*Hearty dish for campers who wake up hungry.*

4 eggs

1 (8-oz.) can whole potatoes, diced

1/2 cup diced cooked ham

1 (2-1/2-oz.) can sliced mushrooms

2 tablespoons milk

1 tablespoon chopped green onion

1/4 teaspoon salt

1/8 teaspoon pepper

2 tablespoons vegetable oil

1/2 cup shredded Cheddar cheese (2-oz.)

Prepare unit for open grilling. In a medium bowl, beat eggs. Stir in potatoes, ham, mushrooms, milk, onion, salt and pepper. Add 1 tablespoon of the oil to preheated grill. Pour half the egg mixture onto grill. Cook until eggs are almost set, about 2 minutes, stirring occasionally. Sprinkle half the cheese on top of the eggs. Cook and stir until eggs are set, about another 1 minute. Repeat, using remaining egg mixture, oil and cheese. Makes 3 to 4 servings.

**Cook the Cheese-Corn Cakes until golden brown on the bottom. Turn and finish cooking.**

## How to Make Cheese-Corn Cakes

# Cheese-Corn Cakes

*The cornmeal flavor goes great with stew.*

1/2 cup cornmeal
1/2 cup all-purpose flour
2 tablespoons sugar
2 teaspoons baking powder
1/4 teaspoon salt
1 egg, beaten

1/2 cup milk
2 tablespoons vegetable oil
1/2 cup shredded process American cheese
    (2-oz.)
1 tablespoon butter or margarine

Prepare unit for open grilling. In a medium bowl, mix cornmeal, flour, sugar, baking powder and salt. Make a well in center. Add egg, milk and oil to well. Stir until just combined. Fold in cheese. On preheated grill, melt butter or margarine. Using 2 tablespoons of batter for each cake, cook cakes 2 at a time until brown, about 1-1/2 minutes on each side. Makes 8 cakes.

1/After grilling the meat, stir together the thawed vegetables, gravy, Worcestershire sauce and Burgundy.

2/Heat the wine-spiked vegetable mixture until bubbly and heated through, then spoon over the meat in bowls.

## How to Make Danish-Style Stew

# Danish-Style Stew

*A hearty stew that's quick-to-fix anytime or anywhere.*

2 tablespoons butter or margarine
8 oz. beef sirloin, cut in strips, 1/4-inch thick
1 (10-oz.) pkg. frozen Danish-style vegetables, thawed

1/2 cup canned mushroom gravy
1 tablespoon Burgundy
1 teaspoon Worcestershire sauce

Prepare unit for open grilling. On preheated grill, melt butter or margarine. Add steak. Cook and stir until done, 3-1/2 to 4 minutes for rare. Place steak in individual serving bowls and keep warm; reserve drippings on grill. In a medium bowl, mix vegetables, gravy, Burgundy and Worcestershire sauce. Add to drippings on grill. Cook and stir until vegetables are done, about 6 minutes. Spoon vegetable mixture over steak in serving bowls. Makes 2 servings.

## Candlelight Dinner for Two

### Menu
*Steak Diane Flambé*
*Boston Lettuce*
*Tomato Wedges*
*Avocado Slices*
*Clear French Dressing*
*Croissants*
*Butter*
*Burgundy*
*Cherries Jubilee*
*Coffee*

**Dazzle your guest with flaming Cherries Jubilee as the grand finale to an exceptional dinner.**

*How to Make Cherries Jubilee*

# Cherries Jubilee

*What could be more impressive than the flaming entree? A flaming dessert!*

1 (16-oz.) can pitted dark sweet cherries
Water, if necessary
1/4 cup sugar
1 tablespoon cornstarch

1 teaspoon lemon juice
3 tablespoons warm brandy
Vanilla ice cream

Prepare unit for open grilling. Drain cherries; reserve syrup. Add water to syrup, if necessary, to make 3/4 cup. In a small bowl or cup, mix sugar and cornstarch. Gradually stir in syrup. Pour onto preheated grill. Cook and stir until thickened and clear, about 2 minutes. Stir in cherries and lemon juice. Unplug grill. Ignite brandy. Pour flaming brandy into sauce. Serve over ice cream when flame subsides. Makes 2 servings.

1/Test the steak for desired doneness by cutting a small slit in the center.

2/Spoon the brandy-spiked mushroom sauce over the steaks just before serving.

## How to Make Steak Diane Flambé

# Steak Diane Flambé

*With your mini-grill on the table, this is a spectacular flaming entrée.*

2 tablespoons butter or margarine
2 (8-oz.) beef rib eye steaks
1/2 cup fresh mushroom slices
1/4 cup chopped onion
1 garlic clove, minced

1/3 cup ketchup
1/2 teaspoon prepared mustard
1/2 teaspoon Worcestershire sauce
2 tablespoons warm brandy

Prepare unit for open grilling. On preheated grill, melt butter or margarine. Place steaks on grill. Cook until brown, about 3 minutes. Turn and cook until done, about 4 minutes for rare. Remove steaks and keep warm. Add mushrooms, onion and garlic to grill. Cook and stir until tender, about 1 minute. Stir in ketchup, mustard and Worcestershire sauce. Cook and stir until heated through, about 1/2 minute. Unplug grill. Ignite brandy. Stir flaming brandy into sauce. Flame will gradually go out. Spoon sauce over steaks. Makes 2 servings.

# Index

# Index